LOC

Touring England by Bus, Boat & Train

THE NORTH COUNTRY

Jean Morris

Local Routes
Touring England by Bus, Boat & Train
The North Country

First edition 2006
ISBN-10: 0-9551940-0-8
ISBN-13: 978-0-9551940-0-9

published in the United Kingdom by
Local Routes
info@localroutes.com
www.localroutes.com

A catalogue record for this book is available from the British Library.

Printed in England by Bemrose Shafron, Chester

Title page photograph Wastwater and The Screes (Tour 6)

This book is dedicated to
Donna Stirling
without whom I would never have had
the courage or conviction to start the project

I would like to thank:
my father, Ronald Morris,
for his blessing
and for reviewing the text,
and
Anne Wilford and Dan Lieberman
for keeping my affairs in order while I was away
and
my honorary aunt,
who regulated my chocolate intake
and was an invaluable sounding board and assistant

Thanks also to
Virgin Trains, First TransPennine Express, Northern Rail, Great North
Eastern Railway and Nexus for their assistance with the train travel

Contents

About Local Routes Travel Guides 5
    About Public Transport 6
    About Accommodation 9
    Especially for Overseas Visitors 11

About Local Routes in The North Country 13
    Getting Started from London and Manchester 14

Important Notes and Useful Tips 15

Tour 1 – Kings, Saints & Vikings: The North-East 17

About Cathedrals and Monasteries 46

Tour 2 – Castles and Abbeys: North Yorkshire 49

Tour 3 –The Eden Valley & West Yorkshire 89

Tour 4 – Hadrian's Wall: Northumberland and Cumbria 117

Tour 5 – The Lake District 145

Tips for Safe Hiking 183

Tour 6 – The Cumbrian Coast 185

Acknowledgements 213

The National Trust 213

English Heritage 213

Useful telephone numbers
and web sites 214

You can still see red squirrels (real
ones) in some parts of Cumbria
(Tours 5 & 6)

About Local Routes Travel Guides

Do you want to explore England without being bound by an organised tour or stressed by overcrowded roads and unfamiliar driving conditions?

If your answer is "yes", then *Local Routes* travel guides are for you!

Each title in the series covers a region of England and contains six **week-long itineraries for tours that can be completed comfortably using public transport**: bus, boat and train. The tours lead you out of the cities and through the countryside to well-known and less-well-known places of great beauty and multi-faceted interest.

England's public transport system has improved greatly over the last few years. Trains are, for the most part, clean, comfortable and punctual – really! Buses, being dependent on traffic conditions, tend to be less punctual, but a few minutes here and there make no difference on these itineraries.

The view from a bus or train is better than from a car, and the would-have-been driver gets to enjoy the scenery, too!

True, some areas are less well served by public transport than others. **The trick is to plan ahead and that is what** *Local Routes* **travel guides do for you**.

Haig Colliery Mining Museum, Whitehaven (Tour 6)

All the tours have been travel-tested by the slightly cranky forty-something author. Each place included meets certain criteria: getting there is stress-free and enjoyable, the route is scenic, the site itself is special, the length of time at the site is neither ridiculously short nor tediously long and carrying luggage is kept to a minimum.

The tours all start and end at a major mainline railway station. They are flexible: you can follow them exactly or modify them to suit your schedule and interests. They include a wide variety of attractions and activities to suit most ages, tastes and interests.

About Public Transport

Local Routes travel guides provide route numbers, frequency of service, length of journey and helpful tips as required. Actual timetables are not provided because they vary with the season.

With this book you can plan your trip ahead then, just prior to heading out, pick up the necessary timetables in any of the following ways:

Those with internet access can download the current timetables via the *Local Routes* companion web site:

www.localroutes.com

Those without internet access can get bus and train departure details on a day by day basis by telephoning:

traveline 0870 608 2 608

This invaluable service (which is not associated with *Local Routes*) takes calls seven days a week from 8.00 to 20.00. Timetables are also available at railway and bus stations and at many Tourist Information Centres (TICs).

Trains

British trains are privately owned. Each company operates a network of routes that are awarded by a process of competitive bidding; therefore, an overlap in service does not usually occur. When it does, the only issue is that timetables published by one train company will not necessarily show all the trains going in your direction. However, many cities and counties publish complete area timetables, and station information boards show all train departures.

On many routes both First and Standard class seating are offered. The difference in comfort is not really worth the extra cost of First; the only real advantage is that you will probably always get a seat without making a reservation.

Since the train trips within each

tour are fairly short, seating should not be a problem – especially if you avoid the second half of July, August and Bank Holiday weekends.

A seat reservation is recommended for long journeys. See page 214 for more information.

Reserved seats are indicated by a card slotted into a holder on the back of the seat or by a scrolling electronic message on the overhead luggage rack. If you can't find a seat, check the cards or messages in case the reservation is for a stretch of journey other than the one you are travelling.

Whenever possible, buy your ticket at the station, rather than on the train, and ask about any specials that might fit your requirements. For example, when a day trip requires a return train journey, you will save money by asking for a "cheap day" or "off-peak" return, but first make sure the time restrictions on the ticket won't interfere with your day: cheap tickets are usually not valid during the early morning and late afternoon peak commuter travel periods.

Only standard tickets are sold on the trains.

A multi-day rail pass is probably only worthwhile for Tour 3 – The Eden Valley & West Yorkshire and Tour 6 – The Cumbrian Coast. The other tours use buses as much as, or more than, trains.

Sometimes specially chartered buses replace trains on weekends due to track maintenance. These buses are clearly indicated, they run from station to station and your train pass or ticket will be valid on them.

On Bank Holiday Mondays trains usually run on the normal Monday schedule.

Buses

Buses are operated by private companies and by town councils. Where several companies operate on a single route they are usually co-ordinated to a single timetable. With buses you can't go too far wrong – you buy your ticket from the driver!

Bus drivers are very helpful people: tell them where you want to go, and they will tell you the best place to get off. Ask the driver to tell you when the bus approaches your stop. Other passengers will often alert you as well.

There are a variety of tickets that can save you money. Tell the bus driver your travel plans for the day and he or she will suggest the best ticket for you.

On Bank Holiday Mondays buses usually run on the normal Sunday schedule.

Motion Sickness Alerts! are included for particularly wobbly journeys. There's nothing like queasiness to spoil an otherwise pleasant drive.

Understanding GETTING THERE
Public transport information is provided in the following format:

> GETTING to WYLAM
> Train d. Newcastle for Wylam Mo-Su 1/hr (15 min)

This means that trains depart Newcastle railway station for Wylam hourly every day. The journey time is about fifteen minutes.

La'al Ratty (Tour 6)

> GETTING to MORPETH
> Bus 416, 516 d. Rothbury Queen's Head for Morpeth Mo-Sa every 2-3 hr; Su/BH every 3-4 hr (40 min)

This means that every two to three hours (every three to four hours on Sunday and Bank Holidays) *either* bus 416 *or* bus 516 leaves Rothbury outside the Queen's Head for Morpeth. Journey time is about forty minutes.

Bank Holidays (BH)
A Bank Holiday is a public holiday. They occur on Good Friday, Easter Monday, the first Monday in May, the last Monday in May and the last Monday in August.

Security on Public Transport
England has been dealing with bomb scares for decades. In the unlikely event of one occurring during your visit, keep calm and follow instructions. Further than that, there are two simple rules:

1) Never leave your luggage unattended. Security personnel may remove and destroy it.

2) If you see an unattended package or bag, ask people in the area if it belongs to them. If it does not, report it immediately to the nearest authority (bus driver, train conductor, station staff, police officer).

About Accommodation

Suggestions for accommodation are listed at the start of each tour. Where available, one is a youth or walkers' hostel; the others are guest houses and inns. Meeting the locals is one of the joys of travel!

Unless otherwise indicated, the listed guest houses and inns have been inspected by at least the local authority (fire and hygiene). Many have also been assessed by the Automobile Association, the Royal Automobile Club or Visit Britain.

The cost per person per night (pppn) for bed and breakfast (full English fry-up or continental) is usually £25.00-£35.00 for singles and £20.00-£30.00 for shared rooms. Prices for family rooms may vary depending on the age and number of the children.

The prices shown are as of September 2005 and are subject to change.

Guest houses are usually family owned, spotlessly clean, comfortable and welcoming. Please note that most, *but not all*, guest houses:

- offer en suite and standard rooms (standard rooms *usually* have their own sink but share a separate toilet and bath/shower)

- cater to special diets with sufficient notice
- provide tea- and coffee-making facilities in, or close to, the bedrooms
- provide a television in every bedroom or in a residents' lounge
- allow all-day access to your room or to a residents' lounge

Some guest houses do not accept children below a given age. Always discuss your requirements and confirm the price with your host when booking.

An inn is a public house that offers accommodation. Some call themselves hotels. Inns offer similar facilities to guest houses but tend to be a bit less personal, a bit noisier and a bit less immaculate (but still clean).

You'll meet all kinds at a Youth Hostel

The following abbreviations are used:
S=single, T=twin, D=double, F=family
T/D=beds convert from twin to double
e=en suite, s=standard, pb=private bathroom, ps=private shower
S in D = single person in double room
pppn = per person per night
For example:
Rooms (£pppn): 1Ss (£25); 2Te/De (£30)
means one single standard room and two en suite rooms that can be twin or double. Cost is £25 and £30 per person per night respectively.

You will also find lists of accommodation at
www.visitbritain.co.uk

Youth Hostels (YHA)

Youth hostels are not just for the young. You don't even have to be a member, but you will be charged an additional fee of £3.00 per night if you aren't.

Whether you are a student, a senior or somewhere in between, there will most likely be others of your age at any of the hostels. Many have family rooms and cots for young children.

For £11 to £20 a night (less if you are under eighteen) you get a bunk in a clean room with one to seven others of your gender. All bedding is provided. Toilets and showers are down the corridor, but you must bring your own towel and toiletries. Towels may be available at reception for a small fee or a substantial deposit.

There will be a well-equipped kitchen for self-catering. Breakfast, a packed lunch and dinner are available at extra cost. The food is usually not bad for mass catering. Exceptions are noted in the listing.

Joining is not expensive (£15.50 in England) and your membership will help keep hostels open. Locate your national hostelling association by visiting
www.hihostels.com.
Prices are for YHA members, adult/under-eighteen as shown:
Cost: £18.00/£13.00
Cost does not include breakfast unless indicated as shown:
Cost: £20.00/£15.00 B&B
Rec.= reception opening hours

YHA Survival Tips

- Book early.
- The online booking system is unreliable. If it says there is no vacancy, try telephoning the hostel directly.
- Your room-mates may snore. Take ear plugs.
- Take flip-flops for the showers.
- Keep valuables with you at all times.

What to pack

Travel light! Keep it down to one small day pack and one piece of luggage. A good backpack is a wonderful thing if you are comfortable with it; otherwise, use something on wheels.

Wear comfortable shoes and plan for layering clothes. A shirt, pullover and lightweight waterproof jacket (with hood) are usually sufficient for the top half. Waterproof trousers make rain almost irrelevant.

Especially for Overseas Visitors

The web site of Visit Britain (once known as the British Tourist Office), provides information on everything from currency to weather:

www.visitbritain.com

When to go

From a weather point of view the best time to visit England is from April to September. October can be good but is more chancy.

Many attractions are closed or have reduced opening hours from November to March. Public transport is also less frequent in many areas during these months.

Attractions, accommodation and public transport are most crowded from mid-July to the end of August.

There are flowers almost year-round, but April is the month for daffodils and lambs.

Personal safety

Leave your valuables and spare credit cards somewhere safe at home. Leave a photocopy of your passport and airplane tickets, a list of credit card and travellers' cheques numbers and the telephone numbers to call in case of theft at home and take copies with you. Carry the copies separate from the originals! If you are travelling with a partner, carry copies of each other's papers as well as of your own.

Carry your money, credit cards and important papers in a safe place: an interior pocket, cotton money belt or similar.

Telephones

To save worrying about correct change for public telephones, buy a telephone card from a post office. The cards come in £5 and £10 denominations and can be used at any telephone: public or private.

Email and internet access

Internet access is available at most libraries for £1.00 per half-hour, but you may need to reserve a time. Some youth hostels have internet access but they are very expensive (7p/minute).

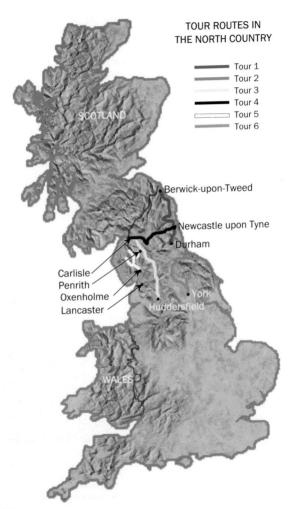

TOUR ROUTES IN
THE NORTH COUNTRY

Tour 1
Tour 2
Tour 3
Tour 4
Tour 5
Tour 6

SCOTLAND

Berwick-upon-Tweed

Newcastle upon Tyne

Durham

Carlisle
Penrith
Oxenholme
Lancaster

York

Huddersfield

WALES

12

About Local Routes in The North Country

England's North Country has an incredible amount to offer visitors. The scenery is bleak and verdant, dramatic and serene; the history reflects the landscape: shaped by farmers, industrialists, writers, philosophers, inventors, engineers, artists, saints (not always saintly) and Vikings (not always vicious).

The tours, each nominally a week long, include stately and not-so-stately homes, formal and country gardens, castles and abbeys, beaches, moors, mountains, lakes and valleys. There is something for everyone.

Tour 1 starts in Berwick-upon-Tweed but immediately heads south to Bamburgh for Lindisfarne and the Farne Islands, then proceeds to Durham with a detour to Alnwick and Rothbury.

Tour 2 is a loop starting at York and extending to the coast at Whitby. It takes in the famous monastic ruins at Rievaulx, Fountains and Mount Grace.

Tour 3 proceeds from Carlisle through the Eden Valley to the northern tip of the Peak District. This tour provides bases for hiking and landmarks of our industrial heritage.

Tour 4 follows Hadrian's Wall from the east coast to Carlisle, with a detour to the northern tip of the Pennines.

Tour 5 covers the Lake District in a series of day trips based at Ambleside, Hawkshead, Keswick, and Glenridding. Hikers can tackle Helvellyn, England's third highest and most-climbed mountain, via Striding Edge from Glenridding or by an easier route from Keswick.

Tour 6 follows the Cumbrian Coast with a detour inland to Wasdale. This tour has an amazing variety of sites and scenery.

A row of 17thC and 18thC tenements backing onto the graveyard at Alston (Tour 4). One shows the telltale bulge of an internal spiral staircase: an unusual feature in such houses.

Getting Started from London and Manchester

Trains depart **London King's Cross** for **Berwick-upon-Tweed** (Tour 1), **York** (Tour 2) and **Newcastle** (Tour 4). Trains depart **London Euston** for **Oxenholme** (Tour 5) and **Carlisle** (Tour 3 and Tour 6).

From **Heathrow** Airport take the *tube* direct to **London King's Cross** (daily 4+/hr, 55 min). From **Gatwick** Airport take the *Thameslink* train to **London King's Cross Thameslink** (which is neither *City Thameslink* nor *King's Cross*) (Mo-Sa 4/hr; Su 2/hr; 45 min).

Euston is about half a mile from King's Cross Thameslink (see the map below).

There are other ways to get to London, but the above routes are easiest to King's Cross and Euston, especially with luggage.

The **British Library**, located half-way between King's Cross and Euston, has a café, washrooms and storage lockers. It also has The John Ritblat Gallery, which includes the Lindisfarne Gospels, Bede's Life of St. Cuthbert, Jane Austen's writing desk, original hand-written lyrics of the Beatles and copies of the Magna Carta. Open Mo, We, Th, Fr 9.30-18.00 Tu 9.30-20.00; Sa 9.30-17.00 Su/BH 11.00-17.00. Cost: free

From **Manchester Airport** or **Piccadilly** take a train direct to **York** or **Oxenholme**. Change at York for **Newcastle** and **Berwick-upon-Tweed**. Change at Preston (on Oxenholme line) for **Carlisle**.

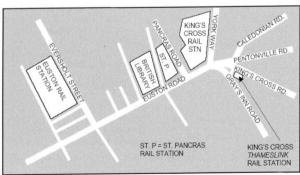

Location of Euston, King's Cross and King's Cross Thameslink railway stations. Not all streets shown. Not to scale.

IMPORTANT NOTES

The information provided in *Local Routes* travel guides is valid from April to October only. Outside these months some public transport services are reduced, some sites have reduced opening hours or are closed and some accommodation is closed. Therefore, "Open daily" applies to April to October, not year round.

Accommodation prices effective as of September 2005. Verify all information and prices with the guest house or inn host prior to making a booking.

Many guest houses and attractions do not accept credit cards.

Most attractions have family rates for admission. The definitions of "family" and "child" vary from place to place. Abbreviations: A=Adult, Ch=Child, Co=Concessions (Seniors, Students, Children depending on attraction). EH=English Heritage property or member, NT=National Trust property or member, YHA=Youth Hostel Association hostel or member, BH=Bank Holiday, SH=School Holiday

Distances are shown in imperial units only. English road signs are in miles, not kilometres.

In the Historical Background sections places in **bold** are visited on the tour.

Although *Local Routes* makes every effort to ensure the accuracy of all the information in this book, changes do occur; therefore *Local Routes* cannot take responsibility for facts, prices, addresses and circumstances in general that are subject to alteration.

USEFUL TIPS

The street plans provided do not show all the streets and are not to scale. Their primary purpose is to locate the rail or bus station and the nearest Tourist Information Centre (shown by *i*), where detailed street plans are available.

Tourist Information Centres are wonderful places: they provide maps and information on local events, special tours and more. They help locate accommodation and provide some public transport information.

Always ask about discounts for National Trust, English Heritage and YHA members and for arriving by bus.

Highlights of Tour 1

- Mainline Rail Station: Berwick-upon-Tweed
  - Three nights in Bamburgh
    - Days 1,2,3 – Travel to Bamburgh for castle. Day trips to Holy Island for Lindisfarne Castle and Priory and to the Farne Islands for birds, seals and St. Cuthbert's hermitage
    - Day 4 – Travel to Rothbury via Alnwick Castle
  - Overnight Rothbury
    - Day 5 – Visit Cragside then continue to Durham
  - Two nights in Durham
    - Days 6,7 – Castle and Cathedral. Day trips to Bede's World and/or Beamish Open Air Museum
- Mainline Rail Station: Durham

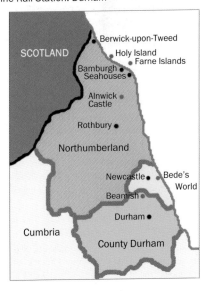

Tour 1 – Kings, Saints & Vikings: The North-East

Grey towers of Durham, yet well I love thy mixed and massive piles,
Half church of god, half castle 'gainst the Scot. Sir Walter Scott

Northumberland's story is one of kings, saints and Vikings; they all descended on Bamburgh, where this tour begins.

This quiet seaside village sits at the foot of a headland topped by Bamburgh Castle. The Farne Islands lie a mile out to sea and Lindisfarne Castle and Priory on Holy Island are a bus ride to the north.

St. Cuthbert ended his 100 years of posthumous travel in Durham, where this tour also ends. In this unpretentious little city are, to my mind, the very best of cathedrals and castles.

Between Bamburgh and Durham are Alnwick Castle and Cragside. Alnwick has a Hogwarts' connection and an extraordinary garden. Cragside was built by a Victorian inventor and is full of wonderful labour-saving devices. Its grounds are less formal than those at Alnwick and offer miles of woodland walks.

Note that there is no access to Inner Farne in October.

Accommodation (see page 10 for abbreviations)

BAMBURGH, Northumberland - 3 nights
Sunningdale Hotel, 21 - 23 Lucker Road, Bamburgh NE69 7BS
Tel. 01668 214 334
E: enquiries@sunningdale-hotel.com   W: www.sunningdale-hotel.com
Rooms (£pppn) 2Se, 2Te, 1Ts, 8De, 5Fe (£27.50-£40 seasonal)

Bamburgh Hall, Bamburgh NE69 7AB
Tel. 01668 214 230; E: creswell@farming.co.uk
W: www.aboutscotland.com/south/bamburgh.html
Rooms (£pppn) 2De, 2Ds, S in D (£40 for 1 night, £30 if 2+ nights)

Glenander, 27 Lucker Road, Bamburgh NE69 7BS
Tel. 01668 214 336
E: enquiries@glenander.com   W: www.glenander.com
Rooms (£pppn) 3De (£27.50-£30)

ROTHBURY, Northumberland - 1 night
Newcastle Hotel, High Street, Rothbury NE65 7UT
Tel. 01669 620 334
Rooms (£pppn) Ss (£30); 3Ts/Ds (£25); 3Te/De (£30), S in D £35

The Haven, Backcrofts, Rothbury NE65 7YA
Tel. 01669 620 577
E: the.haven.rothbury@talk21.com   W: www.thehavenrothbury.co.uk
Rooms (£pppn): 1Se, 3Te, 2De, 1Fe (£35)

Queens Head Hotel, Town Foot, Rothbury NE65 7SR
Tel. 01669 620 470; E: enqs@queensheadrothbury.com
W: www.queensheadrothbury.com
Rooms (£pppn): 3Te, 4De (£30); S in De £42; S in Te £35

DURHAM, County Durham – 2 nights
University of Durham B&B available most of Apr and Jul-Sep
Rooms (£pppn): Approx. 4,000 rooms, S, T, D (£28.50-£40)
E: conference.tourism@durham.ac.uk or Tel. 0191 334 2893

Mrs. T. Koltai, 10 Gilesgate, Durham DH1 1QW
Tel. 0191 386 2026
Room (£/room): 1Ss (£20); 1Ts, 1Ds (£40)

Mrs. J.M. Metcalfe, 12 The Avenue, Durham DH1 4ED
Tel. 0191 384 1020; E: janhanim@aol.com
Rooms (£pppn): 1Ss, 1Ts/Ds/Fs (£21) (2 bathrooms)

Castledene, 37 Nevilledale Terrace, Durham DH1 4QG
Tel. 0191 384 8386
Rooms (£pppn): 2Ts (£20); S in Ts £25-£30

Castle View Guest House, 4 Crossgates, Durham DH1 4PS
Tel. 0191 386 8852
E: castle_view@hotmail.com   W: www.castle-view.co.uk
Rooms (£/room): Se (£45); 2Te, 3De (£70)

Historical Background

The Anglo-Saxons Arrive

In AD409 the Roman empire was collapsing. After almost four centuries of occupation, the legions in Britain were recalled to defend Rome herself from invading Germanic tribes.

Without the legions, the Britons were defenceless against Picts encroaching from the north, so they invited European tribes to settle in Britain in exchange for protection.

Angles and Saxons accepted the invitation and drove the Picts back to Scotland. Then they drove the Britons west to Wales and Cornwall and established their own kingdoms and culture in the new "land of the Angles" or England.

The Kingdom of Northumbria

In 547 an Anglo-Saxon chieftain called Ida became the first king of Northumbria. He built a settlement enclosed within a wooden stockade on an easily defensible headland on a site that had been inhabited since before the Roman occupation.

Ida's grandson, Ethelfrith, gave the settlement to his wife Bebba, hence Bebbanburgh (stronghold of Bebba). Ethelfrith was killed in 616 and his four children escaped to Scotland.

While in Scotland, Ethelfrith's second son, Oswald, met some monks from Iona and converted to Christianity.

Saint Aidan arrives

In 633 Oswald returned to Northumbria as king and established his capital at Bebbanburgh, known to us as **Bamburgh**. Determined to convert his people to Christianity, Oswald sent to Iona for a missionary.

Aidan and twelve monks arrived in 635 and established a monastery at **Lindisfarne**, an island seven miles north of Bamburgh. The monastery comprised a church, workshops and small round huts for the monks. All the buildings had thatched roofs and walls of wood and mud. In the tradition of the Celtic church the monks also built a hermitage on **Inner Farne**, an island facing Bamburgh across a mile of sea. Here the monks retreated for prayer and meditation, free from distraction. "Farne" derives from the Celtic for "a place of retreat".

Aidan was revered for his simple lifestyle, his learning and his kindness. He believed that women could play an important role in the spread of Christianity so he ensured their right to become nuns within Northumbria. It would have been socially unacceptable for women to walk out alone and to speak to strangers, but they could, and did, copy books, study and teach within the confines of their abbey.

Aidan is said to have rescued the stronghold of Bamburgh by changing the direction of the wind when King Penda of Mercia, the kingdom south of Northumbria, tried to set fire to the stockade.

King Penda eventually prevailed, and in 641 killed King Oswald. Oswald was sainted and his head and right hand were preserved at Bamburgh.

Aidan died ten years later in his church in Bamburgh and was sainted.

Saint Cuthbert arrives

Cuthbert was a shepherd of Lammermuir in southeast Scotland. In 651, at the age of seventeen, he was so inspired by a vision of the soul of St. Aidan carried to heaven

Saint Cuthbert with the head of Saint Oswald. From a stained glass window in St. Aidan's Church, Bamburgh

by angels that he became a monk at Melrose Abbey, which had been built by Aidan in 650.

Cuthbert spent some time as guest master in the monastery at Ripon, then returned to Melrose as prior in 661.

Following the Synod of Whitby in 664 (for more on the Synod of Whitby, see page 55), Cuthbert was sent to Lindisfarne as prior with the task of persuading the monks to follow Roman practices rather than those established by St. Aidan.

In 676, Cuthbert followed St. Aidan's example and sought peace and seclusion on Inner Farne. He stayed for nine years until King Egfrith, a nephew of King Oswald,

persuaded him to return to civilisation (and to help sort out the troublesome monk Wilfrid. For more on Wilfrid, see page 55.)

Cuthbert was consecrated Bishop of Lindisfarne on 26 March 685 at York. Two years later, he returned to Inner Farne, where he died on 20 March. His body was buried by the altar of the priory church on Lindisfarne.

Posthumous travels of Saint Cuthbert

Eleven years after Cuthbert's burial the monks of Lindisfarne opened his coffin to put his remains into a small casket on the altar. Instead of the expected dust, they found his body in a remarkably good state of preservation. To

Viking Ship　　　©Regia Anglorum

21

commemorate this apparently miraculous event, Eadrith, Bishop of Lindisfarne, created the Lindisfarne Gospels, 258 pages of exquisite scriptural artwork in the Celtic style, now located in the British Library in London (see page 14).

In 793 Vikings attacked. They swarmed over the island, destroying the church and slaughtering the inhabitants. The few surviving monks rebuilt the church, but, in the face of more Viking attacks in 875, they fled with the body of St. Cuthbert, the head of King Oswald, some bones of St. Aidan and the Lindisfarne Gospels.

For over 100 years the Lindisfarne monks and their successors carried St. Cuthbert's body from place to place, avoiding strife and pillage.

Finally, around 995, they arrived at the site where **Durham** **Cathedral** now stands. Here they built a church and shrine, and here, apart from a short sojourn at Lindisfarne in 1069 to avoid the depredations of William the Conqueror, the body of St. Cuthbert remained.

But not undisturbed. Removed in 1092 to make way for the construction of a Benedictine monastery and cathedral, the body was newly enshrined with the head of St. Oswald in 1104.

In 1540, at the orders of King Henry VIII, the shrine was broken open and the body removed. It was still well-preserved, but this time it was recorded that he had a fortnight's growth of beard. St. Cuthbert was eventually placed were he now rests – under a marble slab in a grandiose chapel behind the altar at Durham Cathedral.

Vikings arrive in Northumbria   ©Regia Anglorum

Day 1 – Arrive and explore Bamburgh

Bamburgh (pr. Bamborough) is located on the Northumbrian coast about sixteen miles south of Berwick-upon-Tweed (Berwick). Access is by bus from Berwick.

"Bleak" best describes the border town of Berwick. It has its charm, albeit well hidden, and should you just miss the bus to Bamburgh you can fill in the time well enough. On a fine day, walking around the Elizabethan ramparts is pleasant and intermittently interesting. If it is raining heavily, which it does in Berwick, frequently, the Barracks offer the regimental museum of the King's Own Scottish Borderers and a very good presentation, *By Beat of Drum*, of life as an infantryman over about 300 years.

Mainline rail station: BERWICK-UPON-TWEED

Exploring Berwick

From the rail station turn right into Castlegate, the main road that leads downhill to the town centre. The TIC is on the left side of Castlegate as you approach the centre. From here you can pick up bus timetables and the tide tables for Holy Island. Turn right into Golden Square, which leads to the Royal Tweed Bridge (built 1928). On the left is a bus stop where you can catch the bus for Bamburgh. Looking from the bridge you can see the Royal Border Railway Bridge (built in 1840 by Robert Stephenson) to the right and Berwick Bridge (built 1624) to the left.

Return to Castlegate (which becomes Marygate at Golden Square) and continue down to West Street. Turn right, towards Berwick Bridge, and follow the lane down to the left. From here you can walk by the river and reach the ramparts. Keep following the ramparts to get to the Barracks.

GETTING to BAMBURGH from BERWICK
Bus 411 d. Berwick rail station and Golden Square for Bamburgh Mo-Sa every 2 hr; Su/BH every 2-3 hr (43 min)

Exploring Bamburgh

This small village is built around a triangular wooded green and is dominated by a massive castle built on an outcrop of rock: the site of Bebbanburgh.

To find the beach, follow the road towards the castle, turn left on the path with a wide playing field on the right, then climb over the sand dunes. The sand stretches as far as the eye can see. On a sunny day it is perfect for walks, games, picnics and sand castles. On wet, windy days it stirs the blood and the imagination.

GOOD EATING

The Copper Kettle makes a very good salad and hot chocolate at a rather steep price.

Fellow travellers recommend *Blacketts Restaurant* on Lucker Road. The food is excellent, the service good and the price reasonable.

St. Aidan's Church

One of Aidan's first tasks on arrival in Bamburgh was to build, with the help of King Oswald, a wooden mission church. It was still standing when Aidan died there in 651, but was later destroyed by fire. Its replacement, also of wood, suffered the same fate, but the third church, built of stone in the late twelfth century, still stands.

Renovated and remodelled over the succeeding centuries, the building shows a mix of Norman and early English architectural styles. The only confirmed remnant of Saxon times is the sundial in the wall of the crypt. However, according to legend, the large wooden beam that is forked at one end and is visible if you look up at

St. Aidan's Church, Bamburgh

24

the baptistery ceiling, was part of the buttress that supported Aidan as he lay dying. It survived the two fires and is said to have miraculous powers.

The church is quite lovely – small and intimate with beautiful stained glass and a magical view from the nave into the chantry.

Grace Darling Museum

Open daily nominally 10.00-17.00
Volunteer-run so hours are variable. Closed for renovation until July 2006.
Cost: free - donation appreciated
Tel. 01668 214465

It is impossible to visit the coast of Northumbria without hearing the story of Grace Darling. On 7 September 1838, at the age of 23, she and her father, the lighthouse keeper on Longstone (one of the Farne Islands), rowed out twice in a strong gale and thick fog to the wrecked steamer Forfarshire to rescue eight men and one woman.

The Grace Darling Museum houses the boat used for the rescue, souvenirs from the time when boats took visitors on celebrity tours to Longstone and other memorabilia.

Grace Darling's grave is in the yard of Saint Aidan's Church.

Bamburgh Castle

Open daily 11.00-17.00
Cost: A £5.50/Co £4.50/Ch £2.50
Tel. 01668 214 515
W: www.bamburghcastle.com

The layout of Bamburgh today reflects the changes brought about by the Norman Conquest. While the Anglo-Saxon kings and commoners had formed a single com-

Bamburgh Castle

munity protected within the walls of the cliff-top fortress, the Normans viewed their rebellious new subjects with distrust and evicted them from the stronghold. The division between castle and village remains.

Under the Normans, Bamburgh, once the proud capital of Northumbria, became just one of many castles constructed for defence against northern invaders.

Over time, the castle fell into disrepair. In the mid-eighteenth century it was restored for use as a girls' charity school and shelter for shipwrecked sailors. In 1894, Lord Armstrong, a solicitor turned engineer, bought the castle to convert into a convalescent home. This project was never completed and it became a private mansion. We will meet Lord Armstrong again at Cragside.

Bamburgh castle is huge and more like a museum than a home, although there are private apartments for the owner and several tenants. The public rooms are on a grand scale and are filled with an eclectic collection of paintings, armour, porcelain and furniture. It all seems a bit soulless, but there are delightful hidden gems of paintings and animal figurines.

The ground floor of the keep is the earliest part of the castle; there is a Saxon well and walls twelve feet thick.

There is the requisite chamber of horrors, which is small but particularly nasty.

All the rooms contain detailed descriptive information.

Included in the price of admission is the **Armstrong Museum,** located in the old laundry buildings of the castle. Lord Armstrong's factories built armaments, ships, bridges, locomotives and hydraulic cranes.

Housed with the Armstrong Museum is the **Bamburgh Castle Aviation Artefact Museum**, which contains memorabilia spanning the history of aviation.

Day 2 – Day Trip to Holy Island

The Normans renamed the island of Lindisfarne "Holy Island" in 1082. The island offers a ruined priory and related museum, an attractive parish church, a gem of a castle, a nature reserve and a pretty little village complete with tea rooms, pubs, craft shops and a mead maker (with free samples).

Holy Island is connected to the mainland by a causeway. This feature complicates getting there somewhat because it is covered at high tide. **Lindisfarne Castle is**

closed on Monday.

GETTING to HOLY ISLAND
First, **check when it is safe to cross the causeway**. The tide table is available at Berwick TIC, hotels and at: www.northumberland.gov.uk/vg /holyisland

Bus 411 d. Bamburgh for Beal (West Mains, Holy Island road end) Mo-Sa every 1-2 hr; Su/BH every 2-3 hr from late a.m. (22 min). The stop is on the church side of the green. Tell the driver you want to go to Holy Island and verify the time of the last bus to Bamburgh.

From Beal (West Mains) it is a good five miles to the village of Holy Island. About three of those miles are under water at high tide, so if you plan to walk, allow plenty of time, as the tide comes in quickly. You probably won't have time to walk and there are other options.

1) Holy Island Mini Bus Service (Tel. 01289 389 236, mobile 0794 9212 527) charge £3.00 per person from Beal, with a minimum charge per trip of £6.00. However, they many not be available when you want them.

2) Fiona Hague (Border Cabs, Tel. 07769 515 915) will pick you up at West Mains and take you to the centre of the village on Holy Island for about £6.70. You can also book her for the return trip to the bus stop.

3) Bus 477 d. Beal for Holy Island Sa & We (daily mid-Jul to Aug) The schedule is tide-dependent; some days the bus cannot run. Visit www.lindisfarne.org.uk/general/ hibus.htm or Berwick TIC for the bus schedule for any given day. If you depend on Bus 477 for a round trip, you may have to stay on Lindisfarne up to seven hours. You will probably find this excessive unless you also want to visit the nature reserve for bird-watching.

You may prefer to cruise from Seahouses with Billy Shiels (Tel. 01665 720 308). Departures are 2/week and coincide with high tide; the castle may not be open. The cruise allows 2 hours on the island, but you can arrange to stay a few days.

Lindisfarne Castle (NT)
Open Tu-Su/BH and first Mo in Aug 10.30-15.00 or 12.00-16.30 to coincide with low tide
Cost: A £5.00/Ch £2.50
Tel. 01289 389 244
E: lindisfarne@nationaltrust.org.uk

The castle is just over half a mile from the village. Walk or take the shuttle service, which makes the round trip every 20 minutes (A £1.30/Ch 90p return). Either way there is a short but steep climb on cobbles to the entrance.

In spite of its location, there does not appear to have been a castle here until the time of Henry VIII, when building began using the stones from the priory. Its original purpose was to provide defence against the Scots and it continued as a garrison thereafter.

It briefly held out for King Charles I against the forces of Oliver Cromwell and even more briefly for King James II (brother of King Charles II), against those of George I, Elector of Hanover. By the early nineteenth the castle had been partially dismantled.

The building was bought by the proprietor of *Country Life* magazine, Edward Hudson, in 1901. He commissioned Edwin Lutyens to restore the castle, not so much as it had been, but as it should have been in the eyes of a serious romantic.

With hugely thick walls and stone floors, the result is everything a castle should be: full of odd little corridors, vaulted ceilings, unexpected stairs and windblown platforms, all on a very intimate and liveable scale: an austere shell with a warm and welcoming interior. My dream home!

Stroll through the field of sheep to visit the walled garden designed and created by Gertrude Jekyll, a gardener, contributor to *Country Life* and frequent collaborator of Lutyens.

Lindisfarne Priory and Priory Museum (EH)

Open daily Apr-Sep 9.30-18.00
Oct 9.30-16.00
Cost: A £3.60/Co £2.70/Ch £1.80
Tel. 01289 389 200

Vikings and time destroyed the original wood and mud monastery of Lindisfarne, but the cult of St. Cuthbert remained strong, particularly at Durham, where his body was finally laid to rest.

Monks travelled from Durham to live as hermits on the Farne Islands, and, towards the middle of the twelfth century, they built a new church at the site of St.

Lindisfarne Castle

Cuthbert's original resting place on Lindisfarne. It is the remains of this church that are visible today.

The church had more than the saint in common with Durham Cathedral: the design and decoration, particularly the incised patterns on the thick Norman columns, are very similar.

The monastic remains date from around 1200, fifty or more years later than the church. The priory would have been a daughter house of Durham.

From the early fourteenth century raiders from the north once again caused strife at Holy Island. Tithes from the parish decreased to about a sixth of their earlier level and the number of monks also decreased. Like Durham, the church became "half church of God, half castle 'gainst the Scot": the walls were strengthened; arrow slits and battlements were added. When the danger passed, windows were incorporated in the church. All these can be seen in the remains.

With the smaller community many of the monastic buildings became redundant and the prior's lodgings became the centre of activity. Lay servants outnumbered the monks by about two to one. The monks enjoyed sports, pubs and naughty jokes, so it should come as no surprise that the abbey

was one of the earliest affected by Henry VIII's dissolution of the monasteries, closing in 1537. For more on the dissolution, see page 57. Stone from the walls was taken to build Lindisfarne castle and, later, for houses and outbuildings by the villagers.

In the early nineteenth century a Mr. Selby bought the property and began to repair the buildings to prevent further damage and decay. The Crown continued this work and the site is now maintained by English Heritage.

The museum provides a good introduction to the history of Lindisfarne: the island and the priory. The gift shop has a fascinating selection of books for all ages, in particular on monastic life.

The Priory itself is in ruins, but enough remains to give a good idea of its structure and the activities within. English Heritage has done a particularly good job with explanatory signs, so it is easy to imagine its former glory.

St. Mary's Parish Church

Although there may have been an earlier building here, the present church dates from 1120 to 1145. The lectern is carved from the pulpit used in the time of Charles I and is the oldest woodwork in the church. The Lindisfarne Gospels inspired the design of the kneelers and the altar carpet. A modern fac-simile of the Lindisfarne Gospels is located in a glass case in the south aisle.

The chancel arch and eastern end of the north arcade have the rounded shape of the Norman pe-riod. The chancel itself and the south arcade are Early English, recognisable by the pointed arch and moderately decorated stone-work. Later still, the arches be-came taller and wider, with highly decorated stonework. For more on church architecture, see page 46.

St. Aidan's Winery

This is simply a shop in the village selling mead and a variety of un-usual fruit wines and spirits as well as biscuits and sweets. Taste a free sample of mead.

Lindisfarne Heritage Centre

Open daily 10.00-17.00
Cost: £2.50/ Under 15 free
Tel. 01289 389 004
W: www.holy-island.info/lhc

Also called the Lindisfarne Gos-pels, Island Life and Nature Exhi-bition. The first of the two rooms

provides several interactive com-puters that let you listen to island-ers' stories and learn about the animals that live there. The second room is devoted to the Lindisfarne Gospels and contains a virtual copy on an interactive screen, as well as a video on the making of a parchment book. Both rooms have puzzles to amuse the children.

Nature Reserve

Holy Island is part of the Lindis-farne National Nature Reserve. While visitors are allowed free ac-cess to the reserve, except certain areas during nesting season, the dunes and marshes are home to several species at risk and care must be taken not to disturb the birds or their habitat. Information and by-laws are posted at the main access points.

RETURN to BAMBURGH
Return to Beal (West Mains) by foot, bus or taxi, and wait by the telephone box half-way between The Plough Hotel and the petrol station for Bus 411 which d. Beal for Bamburgh Mo-Sa every 1-2 hr; Su/BH every 2-3 hr (22 min)

Day 3 – Day Trip to Seahouses for Inner Farne

The Farne Islands, a world of volcanic rock, blustering wind and unsettled water, are home to three- or four thousand grey seals and to many types of seabird, including cormorants, shags, terns, guillemots (pr. "gillymotts"), razorbills and puffins.

The National Trust maintains these islands as a bird sanctuary and only Staple Island and Inner Farne are open to visitors. Access is restricted.

Cruises to the islands operate from Seahouses, a bit of a tacky seaside town. The cruise to Inner Farne, the site of St. Cuthbert's hermitage, passes Longstone, the home of Grace Darling and her father at the time of the Forfarshire rescue.

Tips for the day
- There is no access to Inner Farne or Staple Island in October.
- The last boat to the Farne Islands departs Seahouses at 14.00.
- In rough weather landing on Inner Farne may not be possible. Check with the National Trust (Tel. 01665 720 651 or 01665 721 099) or the cruise operator (Tel. 01665 720 308). Cruises around the islands may continue to operate.
- The smaller excursion boats are open: a pullover, wind/water-proof jacket and sun screen are recommended.
- Don't forget a hat – there are a lot of birds out there!
- *Motion Sickness Alert!*
- The cost of the boat excursion *does not* include the price of landing on Inner Farne. This landing fee is paid directly to the National Trust warden on arrival at the island.

GETTING to SEAHOUSES
Buses 501, 401, 411 d. Bamburgh (opposite the Victoria Hotel) for Seahouses Mo-Sa every 1½ hr; Su/BH every 1¾ hr (9 min). Tell the driver you want to get off for the boat trips.

GETTING to INNER FARNE
via Billy Shiels Boat Trips
Tel. 01665 720 308
W: www.farne-islands.com
The cruise goes around several islands, to see birds and seals, then lands on Inner Farne for about 1 hr. Total length is 2½ - 3 hours.
Cruises for Inner Farne depart Apr, Aug, Sep: 10.00, 11.00, 13.00, 14.00; May-July: 13.00, 14.00

Note: Access to Inner Farne is in the afternoon only during the breeding season from May-July.

Cost: Cruise £8.00 (10% discount for YHA) **plus** landing on Inner Farne (pay the warden on the island):

Apr, Aug, Sep: A £4.00/Ch £2.00
May-July: A £5.00/Ch £2.50

The seam of rock that supports Bamburgh Castle drops abruptly into the North Sea, re-emerges about 1½ miles offshore, then gradually sinks back under the waves, forming a scattering of islands: 15 to 28, depending on the tide.

Inner Farne

The largest island, sixteen acres at low tide, is Inner Farne. St. Cuthbert sought seclusion here for nine years and returned to die in 687.

The island is predominantly igneous (volcanic) rock, with cliffs up to 80 feet high. Just over a quarter of the island is covered by a thin layer of soil, augmented by centuries of bird droppings – enough to support the Elder bushes that were imported by the early lighthouse keepers and an orange wildflower native to California, the Fiddleneck, that was accidentally introduced through poultry feed.

The National Trust provides toilets and a small information centre in the 16th C tower that also houses the wardens for nine months of the year. A path circles the island, passing a 14th C chapel and a 19th C lighthouse.

Just as St. Cuthbert's visitors did over 1,300 years ago and as thousands of pilgrims have since, today's tourists arrive by boat and disembark close to the hermitage guest house or "hospitarium".

St. Cuthbert's spartan cell of wood and thatch no longer stands, but it is likely to have been close to site of the tower, which houses the only well on the island.

After the death of St. Cuthbert pairs of monks inhabited the island. They collected and sold eggs, seal products, fish and ship wreckage to generate sufficient wealth to increase the comforts of the hermitage. Austere St. Cuthbert would not have approved!

Nor would he have approved of the goings-on at the chapel that was built and dedicated to him in 1370. In 1443, the master pawned the best silver and, in 1461, another was rebuked for visiting a woman too frequently. The only remains from this period are the south window and fragments of wall.

In 1538, at the order of King Henry VIII, the islands were handed over to Durham Cathedral. Shortly after, Prior Thomas Castell of Durham built the tower, or "pele", to house the residents of Inner Farne in case of attack from the north.

In the late seventeenth century, a coal fire on the roof of Castell's Tower effectively converted it into a lighthouse. A purpose-built lighthouse with oil-fired lights was built in 1809. The chapel was restored in 1848.

More Cruises from Seahouses
Bird watching on Staple Island (2½ hours, 1 hour on island) or on Staple and Inner Farne (5½ hours, 2 hours on each island).

Grey Seal Cruise (1½ hours, no landings)
Longstone Island to view the lighthouse of Grace Darling fame. (2 hours, with ½ hour landing, no charge for landing as not NT).
Holy Island Cruise (4 hours, with 2 hour landing at high tide). The visit is a bit short to see it all, but has the advantage of fewer visitors: the causeway will be under water.

For more information, call
Billy Shiels
Tel. 01665 720 308
W: www.farne-islands.com

RETURN to BAMBURGH
Buses 501, 401, 411 d. Seahouses for Bamburgh Mo-Sa every 1¾ -2 hr; Su/BH every 2 hr (9 min).

Day 4 – Bamburgh to Rothbury via Alnwick

The route heads inland to Alnwick (pr. "Annick") and to Rothbury, where you will spend the night.

At Alnwick you can visit the castle where Harry Potter had his first flying lesson and wander through the extensive gardens. The town itself is attractive and has some interesting features.

From Alnwick you will continue by bus to the little country town of Rothbury, close to Cragside, the home of Victorian inventor Lord Armstrong, whom you met, figuratively speaking, at Bamburgh Castle. Although the house will be closed for rewiring from September 2005 until spring 2007, the grounds and museum are still well worth a visit.

GETTING to ALNWICK
Bus 501 d. Bamburgh (opposite the Victoria Hotel) for Alnwick daily every 2 hr. For the Gardens tell the driver you want to get off for Alnwick Gardens; otherwise, get off at the bus station. Take the bus that leaves Bamburgh about 10.00 (1¼ hr).

This is a very scenic drive that follows the Coastal Route through many small villages, including Craster, with its tea cup-sized harbour. You can catch a glimpse of Dunstanburgh Castle in the distance.

Alnwick Castle and Gardens
Open Castle daily 11.00-17.00
Garden daily Apr, May, Oct 10.00-18.00; June-Sep 10.00-19.00
Cost: Castle A £7.95/Co £7.50/Ch £2.95
Garden A £6.00/Co £5.75/Ch free
Combined A £12.00/Co £11.50
Tel. 01665 510 777
W: www.alnwickcastle.com

Warning! There is one major set-back to full enjoyment of the castle and grounds: there is nowhere official to leave you luggage. You will have to decide if and where you are prepared to leave it if you want to go inside the castle itself. The security guards are friendly and helpful, but the risk is still all yours. As security is tightening everywhere it is advisable to telephone ahead to verify you can visit the castle interior while leaving your luggage outside.

Alnwick Gardens are spectacular and worth the hefty price of admission, whether you are a keen gardener or just like smelling the roses. There is a Poison Garden (locked, with admission by guided tour only), giant-bamboo labyrinth, rose garden, formal garden, a rather ostentatious cascade and the Serpentine Garden, which is full of wonderful watery surprises.

It all looks a bit too new and raw, as if too much money and expertise are at work conjuring up an almost-instant stately garden. There is none of the mellow settled-in look of a garden allowed to develop with time – but it is still worth the price of admission!

Alnwick is the second largest inhabited castle in England (after Windsor) and has been home to the Percy family, Earls and Dukes of Northumberland, since 1309.

Although the earliest reference to the castle is from 1096, the first Percy undertook some major restoration work, and there have been many additions and modifications since. The most recent addition, a Knights School, opened in 2005.

Alnwick is even grander than Bamburgh but, although the state rooms were extravagantly and elegantly restored and refurnished in the mid-nineteenth century, it still looks as if someone might actually live there, as, in fact, the Duke and Duchess of Northumberland do.

Parts of *Harry Potter and the Philosopher's Stone* were filmed in the bailey, and you might still see a Gryffindor or two stroll by.

GOOD EATING

Buy the makings for a picnic lunch from one of the bakers in Alnwick and enjoy it by the castle on the vast expanse of grass that overlooks the landscape of Capability Brown.

The town of Alnwick

There is more to Alnwick than the castle and gardens. Apart from good bakers, there are 16thC alms houses, a row of cottages designed by Edwin Lutyen's son, Robert, and a 15thC church. You can also take a look at a suite from the R.M.S. *Olympic*, sister ship to the *Titanic*, now in the White Swan.

Alnwick is the home of Barter

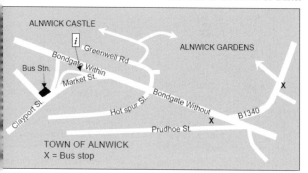

ALNWICK CASTLE

i

Greenwell Rd

ALNWICK GARDENS

Bondgate Within

Bus Stn.

Market St.

Clayport St.

Hot spur St.

Bondgate Without

B1340

Prudhoe St.

TOWN OF ALNWICK
X = Bus stop

Books (open daily 9.00-17.00), one of the largest second-hand bookshops in Britain. And only in Alnwick will you find a Hairy Lemon and Jimmy's Dribble.

Saturday is market day. The last Friday of each month is a Farmers' Market.

If you visit the garden first, you can detour to the town centre (signposted along the path from the garden to the castle) then continue towards the castle. Your ticket gives you entry to the grounds throughout the day.

Continue to Rothbury.

GETTING to ROTHBURY
The trip requires a change of bus at Morpeth, an attractive little market town. You will have anywhere from 10 minutes to an hour in Morpeth between buses. If time is particularly tight, the change can be made at Lancaster Park Estate entrance (shortly after the bus turns off the A1 towards Morpeth), otherwise change at Morpeth bus stn.

Bus 505, 515 d. Alnwick bus stn for Morpeth Mo-Sa 1/hr (45 min)
Bus 525 d. Alnwick bus stn for Morpeth Su every 1-2 hr (46 min)
Bus 416, 516 d. Morpeth bus stn

Armstrong Cottages, Rothbury

for Rothbury via Lancaster Park Estate entrance Mo-Sa every 1½-3 hr; Su 3/day (40 min)

Note: About 16.00 there will be several school buses passing Lancaster Park Estate entrance. They do not have numbers. The bus you want is clearly identified.

The trip from Morpeth to Rothbury is very scenic. It moves into higher and more wooded ground than previously and runs by a river.

Rothbury was officially granted market town status by King John in 1291. It lies beside the River Coquet, which is spanned by a 15thC pack-horse bridge with one 18thC arch.

Lord Armstrong (of Bamburgh and Cragside) is buried in the church cemetery, where the oldest headstones are from the seventeenth century.

The church is the usual mix of styles and was much renovated in the nineteenth century, but the pedestal of the baptismal font is from the shaft of an 8thC Anglo-Saxon cross and includes a relief of the Ascension, possibly the earliest depiction of this in England.

The market cross was built in 1902 in the style of the Arts & Crafts movement (see page 159).

If you enjoy walking, you may want to stay longer than one night to explore Coquetdale and the Northumberland National Park. The TIC has several leaflets describing a range of walks.

Overnight in Rothbury

Day 5 – Cragside and Durham

Leave your luggage at your guest house to collect later and enjoy a day at Cragside.

Cragside House is located about 1½ miles north-east of Rothbury. It was the first house in the world to be served by hydro-electricity. Unfortunately, its wiring has not been updated since, so it will be closed for about 18 months from September 2005.

However, the visitor centre, Armstrong Gallery, gardens and grounds will remain open and you can happily spend at least a morning exploring before enjoying a Victorian lunch at the restaurant.

In the afternoon, collect your bags and start out for Durham.

THE WALK to CRAGSIDE
Walking uphill to Cragside is unavoidable, whether by road or footpath. The road is narrow and busy, but has better footing and is less steep than the footpath. The riverside stretch of the footpath is more attractive and safer, but the uphill stretch may be muddy or

slippery.

BY ROAD

Follow the main road downhill out of Rothbury, following the signpost to Cragside. On the left you will pass an idyllic little cluster of cottages around a green. These were built by Lord Armstrong in memory of his mother. Once outside the village, the road forks: take the left hand road (B6341) uphill and follow it about 1¼ miles to Cragside, on the right. Keep well to the right side of the road as it is narrow, hilly and twisty.

BY FOOTPATH

Turn down Bridge Street and follow the path down to the river immediately to the left of the bridge. Turn left and proceed along first a "private" road (open to pedestrians), then a paved road until you reach the Northern Area Rothbury Depot. Follow the footpath beside the river until you reach a busy road.

Turn right at the road, over the bridge and immediately on your left is a stone house with a steep roof. This is Burnfoot House on the Cragside Estate. Exercise extreme caution crossing the road.

Turn left up the drive and follow the path past the house and additional buildings (the Cragside Power House). You will start to

see signs leading to 'House'. Where the path splits near the Waterwheel, take the left fork for the official entrance, about ¾ to 1 mile north, to purchase your entry ticket and receive a map of the estate.

Lord Armstrong

William Armstrong was born in Newcastle in 1810. His father was a corn merchant who became Mayor of Newcastle in 1850 and his mother was the daughter of a colliery owner. At his father's wishes, Armstrong read law but studied and experimented with mechanics in his free time.

In 1845 he developed a system whereby reservoirs about 200 feet higher above sea level than Newcastle supplied the city with water at a consistently higher pressure than had been possible with the local supply. He then used the water supply to power new cranes at Newcastle docks.

In 1847 Armstrong gave up law and founded W. G. Armstrong & Company. He designed a hydraulic accumulator to further increase and maintain water pressure for industrial use. His company supplied the hydraulic lifts for Tower Bridge in London.

W.G. Armstrong & Company designed a breech-loading (instead of muzzle-loading) gun with a rifled barrel (a spiral is machined along the interior of the barrel to give a spin to the projectile, making it more accurate). As a result, Armstrong was knighted and appointed Chief Engineer of Rifled Ordnance and Superintendent of the Royal Gun Factory at Woolwich. He was also chairman of the Whittle Dean Water Company and President of the Institution of Mechanical Engineers.

In 1862 W.G. Armstrong & Company took economic advantage of the American Civil War by selling guns to both sides.

In 1863 Armstrong began building Cragside, where he used his expertise in hydraulics to increase efficiency in both the house and the estate, most famously for generating electric light.

In 1887 he became the first Baron Armstrong of Cragside. Lady Armstrong died childless in 1893, so when Lord Armstrong died in 1900 his nephew inherited the estate.

Cragside (NT)

The house will be closed from 25 September 2005 for 18 months for complete rewiring. The grounds, gardens and Stables Visitor Centre, including the shop, restaurant and Armstrong Gallery, will remain open as usual.

Open House Tu-Su/BH 13.00-17.30

Grounds and Estate Tu-Su/BH 10.30-19.00 (or dusk if earlier)

Shop and Restaurant 10.30-17.30

Cost: House, Gardens & Estate A £8.50/Ch £4.00

Gardens & Estate A £5.70/Ch £2.60

Tel. 01669 620333/620150

E: cragside@nationaltrust.org.uk

A good day's outing is to arrive about 10.30 to explore the grounds and gardens, then break for lunch before viewing the house, if it is open, or exploring Rothbury.

Lady Armstrong was interested in botany and played a major role in the planting of the grounds. One of the largest rock gardens in Europe surrounds the house and the tallest Douglas Fir in England thrives in the forest. There are formal gardens and stone grottoes oozing dripping ferns. There is an orchard house with a variety of citrus fruit trees. There are waterfalls and pools, a clock tower, pump house, power house and a single-span iron footbridge. There are over forty miles of paths to explore!

The house, a massive Victorian folly rising above the evergreen forest and backed against a craggy hillside, looks quite Ruritanian.

The interior, an exuberant example of Victoriana, offers, among much else, a fabulous nursery and pre-Raphaelite textiles, wallpaper and stained glass. Lord Armstrong's inventions are at work throughout, especially in the kitchen. There are explanatory notes in each room and the room stewards are very knowledgeable.

GOOD EATING

Traditional Victorian food is served at the *Stables Restaurant* from 12.00-14.00. The food is good, the restaurant is licensed and you can sit inside or in the courtyard.

Next to the Stables Restaurant is the Armstrong Gallery. This excellent display explains in simple terms the engineering principles behind Lord Armstrong's inventions.

Return to Rothbury to collect your luggage. Proceed to Durham.

GETTING to DURHAM

Bus 416, 516 d. Rothbury (outside Queen's Head Hotel) for Morpeth and Newcastle Haymarket bus stn Mo-Sa every 2-3 hr, Su 3/day (change at Morpeth for connecting bus to Newcastle). There is one bus in the afternoon that goes direct to Newcastle Haymarket bus station on Mo-Sa.

From Newcastle Haymarket follow signs to Metro (black M in yellow square) and travel two stops south on either the yellow or green line to Newcastle Central Station (all within Zone 1)

Trains d. Newcastle Central Station for Durham daily 3+/hr (14 min)

Day 6 – Durham

It is likely that Durham castle and cathedral will be the highlights of your trip.

While the city's shell is the usual bleak, blocky, sharp-edged *ugliness*, Durham's heart is, thank goodness, enclosed and protected by the River Wear, as it has been since its founding over 1,000 years ago.

Its founding was the result of St. Cuthbert (deceased), some monks from Lindisfarne, two milkmaids and a dun cow. It seems that the monks, who had been carrying St. Cuthbert's coffin around the north of England for close to 100 years, had a bit of a rest near the River Wear. When they prepared to trudge onward, the coffin refused to move until two milkmaids looking for a dun cow walked by. The monks followed the maids, the coffin consented to go with them and they all settled down at Dun Holm.

Durham Castle

Open Easter-Sep a.m. & p.m. daily; Apr&Oct p.m. only Mo, We, Sa, Su Access by guided tour only. Tour times are posted by entrance. Reservations are not required, but the castle is sometimes closed for special events. Check with the castle porter (Tel. 0191 334 3800)
Cost: A £5.00/Co £3.00/Ch £2.50
W: www.durhamcastle.com

Durham was one of William the Conqueror's northern strongholds. He gave custody of the castle to the Bishop of Durham and it remained a bishop's palace until 1837. Since then it has been a residential college of the University of Durham.

Because Durham's bishops combined their spiritual role with the administrative, military and judicial powers associated with custody of an important castle, they were designated Prince-Bishops.

It is possible to trace the evolution of the site from the basic motte and bailey of its origins to the grandiose palace of today. There is no record of Durham castle ever being taken by force.

Highlights of the tour include a 17^{th}C black oak cantilevered staircase (unfortunately, it was so heavy that it was in danger of pulling the wall down, so additional columns were added), a well-preserved and beautifully carved

Norman doorway and an 11^{th}C chapel, complete with pagan-looking capitals.

Durham Cathedral

Open daily. Access restricted during services and evening recitals.
Cost: Free except the Treasures of St. Cuthbert, Tower and Monks' Dormitory
Tel. 0191 386 4266
W: www.durhamcathedral.co.uk

Durham Cathedral is possibly the finest example of late Norman ar-

Statue of the Third Marquess of Londonderry in Durham Market Place

41

chitecture in the world. It is magnificent.

This is the culmination of St. Cuthbert's story: his tomb is in a shrine behind the altar. A black marble line, which is still visible on the floor, defined the nearest women were allowed to approach. Although Cuthbert was known for his talents of healing and prophecy, his kindness and patience, his teaching and his ministry to the poor, sick and bereaved, he is supposed to have disliked women.

His dislike was so strong that when cracks appeared in the ground during construction of a Lady Chapel close to his shrine it was thought wise to relocate the chapel to avoid his displeasure.

Take time to explore the cathedral. There is so much to see, from the first awe-inspiring view down the nave to the detailed carvings on the misericords. The Treasury displays St. Cuthbert's jewelled cross, which was found in his coffin, while the Library in the original Monks' Dormitory houses more fascinating items.

The Venerable Bede, who was never here in his lifetime, rests in the Galilee chapel, a victim of the morbid taste for bones indulged in by certain members of the clergy. In this instance it was the sacristan of Durham Cathedral who stole the bones from their original resting place in Jarrow in 1022.

GOOD EATING

Opposite the Treasury, in the Monks' Wine Cellar, a self-service restaurant offers good, imaginative food at a fairly reasonable price.

After lunch, exit the cloisters, turn right (noting the octagonal water tower built 1751 on the left) and

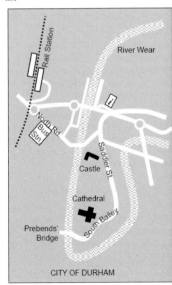

CITY OF DURHAM

leave the courtyard through the steep narrow passage. Turn left and follow the path downhill, around a hairpin bend and down some steps on the left. At the bottom of the steps turn right to visit the small **Archaeology Museum**
Open daily 11.00-16.00
Cost: A £1/SrCh 50p

or continue uphill on the left-hand path. Cross the Prebends' Bridge, turn right and follow the riverside footpath for some lovely views of the cathedral.

If you return over the Prebends' Bridge and follow the road, you will eventually arrive at St. Mary le Bow church, which now houses:

The Durham Heritage Centre and Museum
Open Apr, May, Oct: Sa, Su/BH 14.00-16.30; Jun: daily 14.00-16.30; Jul-Sep daily 11.00-16.30
Cost: A£1.20/Co 80p/Ch 50p
Tel. 0191 386 8719/384 5589

The museum uses a variety of displays to present the social history of Durham from its founding to the present. Coal mining was a major industry; carpet and organ manufacture are ongoing. Sadly, brewing is not.

Day 7 – Day Trip to Bede's World

If you have time, a visit to Bede's World will help round out your knowledge of Anglo-Saxon life in England. This attraction includes an "Anglo-Saxon" farm and village as well as a museum.

The Venerable Bede was born about 673 in Northumbria. From the age of seven he lived in the twin monasteries of Jarrow and Monkwearmouth. He was a student of history and wrote several books, including his most famous work, *The Ecclesiastical History of the English People,* which is a primary source for knowledge of his times.

Bede died in 735 and was buried at Jarrow. In 1022 his remains were stolen and are now at Durham Cathedral.

The outing includes a visit to St. Paul's Church, which is attached to the rather scanty remains of Bede's monastery of Jarrow.

GETTING to ST. PAUL'S CHURCH
Trains d. Durham for Newcastle daily 3+/hr (14 min)

In Newcastle rail stn follow the Metro signs to the platform for the green line train for South Shields. Do *not* take the train for South Hylton, which leaves from the same platform. The destination of the trains is shown on the front of each and on an electronic sign on the platform, which also indicates how soon the next two or three trains will arrive.

Alight from the Metro at Jarrow for a bus to Bede's World, or at Bede to walk.

Buses 526, 527 d. Jarrow Metro stn daily 4/hr at alternating intervals of 8 and 22 min (5 min)

To walk, exit Bede station and turn left (signposted to Bede's World). The Barbour Factory Outlet should very quickly appear on your left. At the T-junction turn left and follow the road as it swings to the right to intersect with the busy A185. Cross A185 and continue to the left. After the timber yard on the right, turn right. You will cross a bridge over the Don River and come to a sign on your right to St. Paul's Church. About 20 minutes' walk.

St. Paul's Parish Church

St. Paul's Church was part of the monastery at Jarrow where the Venerable Bede lived. It was built in AD681, and retains more than the usual amount of its original structure: the chancel is Saxon and the small middle window on the south wall is Saxon glass. Within the sanctuary of the chancel is an ancient chair, supposedly Bede's.

Most of the remainder of the church is Victorian, but there is a display of Saxon stonework along the north wall of the nave. Some ruins of the monastery are adjacent to the church.

GETTING to BEDE'S WORLD
From St. Paul's Church walk across the wide green of Drewett's Park, passing some swings on your left, towards the large brick building at the top of a flight of steps. Go to the left of the brick building and ahead is the entrance to Bede's World.

Bede's World

Open Mo-Sa 10.00-17.30
Su 12.00-17.30. Closed Good Friday
Cost A£4.50/Co £3.00
EH members 50% discount
Tel. 0191 489 2106
W: www.bedesworld.co.uk

The museum is airy and spacious, informative and enjoyable. In particular, the Anglo-Saxon farm provides a nice walk with reconstructed houses, early breeds of farm animals and cultivated plants and a good view of the Tyne from the surrounding bank.

Additional Day Trip

The North of England Open Air Museum at Beamish makes an enjoyable day trip and is easily reached by bus from Durham. There is a tea room, coffee shop and pub, or take a picnic to eat on the town green. See page 126 for more information on the museum.

GETTING to BEAMISH
Bus 720 d. Durham Bus Station
Mo-Su 1/hr (33 min) Return stop
is about 50 yard past the Shepherd and Shepherdess pub

For more things to do around Newcastle see pages 122 to 128.

Getting Home

Durham is on the mainline to York from where you can catch a train to London, Manchester or just about anywhere else.

About Cathedrals and Monasteries

A **cathedral** is a church that is the *seat* or headquarters of a bishop. It is where his throne (or seat) is located.

Churches and monasteries are governed by a **chapter**. In a monastery the chapter consists of the abbot and monks. In a non-monastic (**collegiate**) church the chapter consists of **canons**. The chapter meets in the **chapter house**, which is usually round or octagonal with ornate stonework. Chapter houses are usually well worth a visit.

In a monastic church the monks use the **choir** (hence the term "choir monks"), which is isolated from the **nave**. The nave is where the lay brothers pray. For more on lay brothers, see page 54.

The diagram below shows the main areas of a church or cathedral. There are usually some chapels in the **transepts** and the **chancel** aisles. A tower often stands over the **crossing**. In several churches, such as Selby (Tour 2), the weight of the tower on poor foundations has caused the crossing and adjacent arches to deform.

Monastic buildings were usually built to the south of the church. Of the full range of buildings, only the **cloister** is shown below. In monastic churches, such as at Cartmel (Tour 6), you may see the night stair (used by monks to get from the dormitory to the choir for night services) in the south transept.

Monasteries in the care of English Heritage have excellent information boards that illustrate the layout of each site in detail.

Benedictine abbeys were built

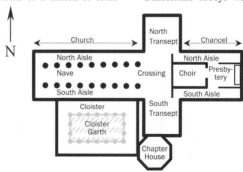

near towns and, in some places, the local people used the nave as their parish church. Because of this, most monastic churches that are still in use were attached to Benedictine abbeys.

Old churches, cathedrals in particular, are fascinating and fun places to visit. Carvings on the misericords (the monks' seats in the choir) are always worth checking out. The early craftsmen weren't necessarily always Christian and some had a wicked sense of humour that sometimes ran wild in less visible areas! For the same reason, take a good look at the ceiling bosses and column capitals.

Glossary

chantry: a chapel within a church, used for saying masses for the soul of the donor

cloister: a covered area around an open court (or cloister **garth**). Monks often studied in carrels in the cloisters as they provided light and some protection from the weather.

grange: farm owned by an abbey and worked by the abbey's lay brothers

Lady chapel: chapel dedicated to Mary, mother of Jesus

minster: the Anglo-Saxon evangelists worked from a base in an urban centre. Satellite churches developed as the rural areas converted. The clergy of the satellite churches were under the authority of the urban church or **minster**, which was within the diocese of, and under the authority of, a bishop. Anglo-Saxon minsters were served by priests, not monks. **York Minster** is, strictly speaking, a cathedral, being the seat of the archbishop of York, but it retains its Anglo-Saxon name of minster.

see: an ecclesiastical area under the jurisdiction of a bishop or archbishop

mother house: an established monastery from which monks went out to found new monasteries

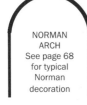

NORMAN ARCH
See page 68 for typical Norman decoration

See page 59 for more on cathedral architecture.

EARLY ENGLISH ARCH

Highlights of Tour 2

- Mainline Rail Station: York
  - York – prelude to tour
    - York Minster, Castle Howard and Selby Abbey
    - Day 1 of tour– Travel to Ripon for Cathedral
  - Two nights in Ripon
    - Day 2 –Fountains Abbey & Studley Royal
    - Day 3 – Travel to Thirsk for World of James Herriot then to Osmotherley for Mount Grace Priory
  - Overnight in Osmotherley
    - Day 4 – Travel via Ormesby Hall to Whitby
  - Two nights in Whitby
    - Day 5 – Whitby Abbey, seaside and Robin Hood's Bay
    - Day 6 – Travel via North Yorkshire Moors Railway to Pickering for Camp Eden. Proceed to Helmsley
  - Two nights in Helmsley
    - Helmsley Castle, Rievaulx Abbey, Duncombe Park
- Mainline Rail Station: York

Tour 2 – Castles and Abbeys: North Yorkshire

Rievaulx Abbey

York is the beginning and the end of this circuit of north Yorkshire. It is a beautiful city and knows it! It is also easily reached by train from just about anywhere.

Since you will probably want to spend a few days in York before heading out to the moors, some of the many attractions in and around the city have been included as a prelude to the tour.

From York a circle west to Ripon, north to Osmotherley, east to Whitby and back to York via Helmsley encompasses some of the most beautiful abbey ruins in England, set among rolling hills and wooded valleys.

Although the theme of this tour is Monastic Yorkshire, there is much more: the ultimate stately home at Castle Howard, equally stately gardens, the seaside, a war museum in an old prisoner-of-war camp, a smugglers' village, Roman baths, a medieval Little Ease prison, Captain Cook's house, James Herriot's house and fossils of Jurassic reptiles.

Accommodation (see page 10 for abbreviations)

YORK, North Yorkshire
YHA, Water End, Clifton, York YO30 6LP
Tel. UK 0870 770 6102; Int (+44) 1904 653 147
E: york@yha.org.uk
Cost: £18.00/£13.00 B&B
Open daily; Rec. 7.00-23.30
Half-hour walk from York rail station. During my stay the food was the worst kind of institutional. Bring your own evening meal or eat out.

Greenside Guest House, 124 Clifton, York YO30 6BQ
Tel. 01904 623 631
E: greenside@amserve.com   W: www.greensideguesthouse.co.uk
Rooms (£/pppn): 3Ss (£25); 3Ds/Ts/Fs, 4De/Te/Fe (£22+)
About 25 minutes' walk from York rail stn.

GETTING to YHA and Greenside Guest House
First Park&Ride Bus 2 (Green Line) d. Station Ave. Mo-Su 6/hr. Stops at Clifton Green, two minutes' walk to Greenside and about five to YHA

Georgian House Hotel, 35 Bootham, York YO30 7BT
Tel. 01904 622 874
Rooms (£pppn): 1Se (£40), 8De, 4Te, 3Fe (£24-£30)
No children under five

RIPON, North Yorkshire - 2 nights
Crescent Lodge, 42 North Street, Ripon HG4 1EN
Tel. 01765 609 589
E: simpgry@aol.com   W: www.crescent-lodge.com
Rooms (£/room): 1Se (£32); 1Te, 2De (£50); 5Fe (£60+)

Riverside, 20—22 Boroughbridge Road, Ripon HG4 1QW
Tel. 01765 603 864
Room (£pppn): 1Ss, 1Ts (£24); 2Se (£30); 5Te/5De (£26), 3Fe

The White Horse, 61 North Street, Ripon HG4 1EN
Tel. 01765 603 622
Rooms (£/room): 4Se (£30); 4Te (£50); 4Fe (£50+)

OSMOTHERLEY, North Yorkshire – 1 night
YHA, Cote Ghyll, Osmotherley DL6 3AH
Tel. UK 0870 770 5982; Int (+44) 1609 883 575
E: osmotherley@yha.org.uk
Cost: £11.00/£8.00

Open Apr-Jun, Sep, Oct flexible, Jul, Aug daily
Rec. 7.00-10.00, 17.00-22.30   Laundry

Queen Catherine Hotel, 7 West End, Osmotherley DL6 3AG
Tel. 01609 883 209; E: queencatherinehotel@yahoo.co.uk
W: www.queencatherinehotel.co.uk
Rooms (£pppn). 2Se, 2Te, 1De (£25)

Vane House, 11A North End, Osmotherley, DL6 3BA.
Tel. 01609 883 448
E: allan@vanehouse.co.uk   W: www.vanehouse.co.uk
Rooms(£pppn): 4Te, 3De, 1Fe (£30); S in D £30

WHITBY, North Yorkshire – 2 nights
YHA, East Cliff, Whitby YO22 4JT
Tel. UK 0870 770 6088; Int (+44) 1947 602 878
E: whitby@yha.org.uk
Cost: £11.00/£8.00
Open daily Apr-Aug, Mo-Sa Sep-Oct, Rec. 8.00-10.00, 17.00-22.00

Kimberley House Hotel, 7 Havelock Place, Whitby YO21 3ER
Tel. 01947 604 125; E: enquiries@kimberleyhouse.com
W: www.kimberleyhouse.com. Very friendly and helpful.
Rooms (£/room): 1Sps (£22); 2Te/Fe, 5De (£25) S in D £30

Havelock Guest House, 30 Hudson St., Whitby, YO21 3EP
Tel. 01947 602 295; E: havelock30@aol.com
Rooms (£pppn): 5Ss, 1Ds (£19.50); 1Te, 5De, 1Fe (£22)

HELMSLEY, North Yorkshire – 2 nights
YHA, Carlton Lane, Helmsley YO62 5HB
E: helmsley@yha.org.uk
Cost: £12.50/£9.00
Tel. UK 0870 770 5860; Int (+44) 1439 770 433
Open Apr-Jun, Sep, Oct. flexible; Jul, Aug daily
Rec. 8.00-10.00, 17.00-22.00
Definitely one of the better YHA dinners!

Crown Hotel, Market Square, Helmsley YO62 5BJ
Tel. 01439 770 297
Rooms (£pppn): 2Se, 5Te, 4De, 1Fe (£38)

The Carlton Lodge, Bondgate, Helmsley YO62 5EY
Tel. 01439 770 557
E: welcome@carlton-lodge.com   W: www.carlton-lodge.com
Rooms (£pppn): 1Se (£40); 5Te/De, 1De, 1Te (£35); S in D £45

Historical Background

Records from 1,500 years ago are fragmentary, to say the least, and sometimes conflicting; however, I hope this brief history will help you to build your own picture of Anglo-Saxon and Norman Yorkshire. To start at the very beginning, first read the historical background to Tour 1.

A Bit About Monks

At first the term "monk" had no real definition. Monks could live alone or in monastic communities. There were no orders and no standards. The followers of St. Benedict were to change all that.

Benedictines

St. Benedict, the "Patriarch of Western Monasticism", never intended to start a new monastic order. When he wrote what is now

Monk at work
©Regia Anglorum

called *The Rule of St. Benedict* in the early sixth century he only wanted to lay down some guidelines for monastic life in general. It was some time after his death that the abbeys following his Rule were dubbed Benedictine.

The Rule of St. Benedict states that a monk's life should be dedicated to prayer, study and manual labour. Benedictine abbeys accumulated large libraries and extensive estates. They reclaimed wasteland for growing crops and breeding cattle, horses and sheep. They built sophisticated plumbing with running water, filter tanks and drains. They provided education for the rich, alms for the poor, hospitals for the sick and lodging for travellers.

Monks being human, some monasteries became lax in their discipline and corrupt in their power. A few dedicated monks left to form more austere communities, some of which developed into new monastic orders.

Carthusians

In 1084 one such community began at Grande Chartreuse. The monks chose an eremitic, or hermit-like, life: isolated, self-centred and altogether less useful than that suggested by Benedict. Each lived in his own "cell" within the monastery enclosure and spent most of his time in private meditation and prayer.

The movement grew and, inevitably, an Organiser emerged. Guigues du Pin drew up a set of rules which were approved by Pope Innocent II in 1133. The new organisation was called the Sacred Eremitic Carthusian Order.

The Carthusian order strikes one as staggeringly selfish, "for it was not for the temporal cure of other folk's bodies, but for the welfare of our own souls, that we took refuge in the retirement of this desert." (Guiges du Pin)

While the Benedictines were a vital part of the surrounding communities, the Carthusians built in isolated areas, turning their back on the local peasantry.

At **Mount Grace Priory** you will see that for all the supposed austerity and simplicity of their lives, each Carthusian monk had his own cosy little cottage with a fireplace in the parlour, a bedroom with curtained bed (to keep out the draughts), a study, a workroom and a private loo reached by a covered passage. Vegetarian meals were delivered by lay brothers through a hatch in the wall. Behind each cottage was a pleasant little walled garden.

Only three of the seven daily services were celebrated in the church: matins, high mass and vespers. One wonders how many of the monks slept through the night services they were supposed to celebrate in their cells.

The Carthusians took their plumbing seriously so it is safe to assume the monks were cleaner and healthier as well as more comfortable than the majority of people at the time.

Cistercians

In 1098 another group of unhappy Benedictines left their abbey in Molesme to start a new life following the Rule of St. Benedict in Cistercium (Cîteaux, France).

As Cistercium grew, groups of monks left to establish "daughter" monasteries. By 1119 a total of ten

Ornate ironwork on Selby Abbey door

existed and a new order, called Cistercian, was recognised.

Their ideals were simplicity, poverty and isolation. They wore wool gowns over bare flesh, ate no meat and devoted themselves to prayer, study and labour.

As the order gained in popularity, so it gained in wealth. In the absence of poverty, simplicity and isolation retreated. The monks restricted their labour to study and prayer, leaving the hard work to lay brothers.

Lay brothers were drawn from the peasantry and became the skilled tradesmen and farmers of the Cistercian abbeys. They took monastic vows but were strictly segregated from the aristocratic choir monks. They ate and slept in separate quarters and had their own altar in the church nave rather than contaminate the church choir with their presence.

On the other hand, lay brothers ate and slept more than the choir monks because they had to work harder, and they were able to leave the abbey to work at the outlying farms or granges.

The Cistercians extended their estates by relocating villages, dispossessing peasants and reclaiming wasteland. As the abbeys became more involved in industry and agriculture, their churches be-

came more ornate – statements of their wealth and power. The Cistercian abbeys at **Rievaulx** and **Fountains** hardly reflect simplicity and poverty!

The Anglo-Saxons

With the departure of the Roman legions in AD410 Christianity in England lay dormant until 596, when Pope Gregory sent Augustine to convert the Anglo-Saxons to the church of Rome.

Augustine started with King Ethelbert of Kent, whose wife was Christian, then converted the majority of the southern Anglo-Saxons before dying in 604 as Archbishop of Canterbury.

He had been less successful wooing the Celtic Christian church that had returned to Ireland with St. Patrick in 432 and had arrived in Scotland with St. Columba in 565. The Celtic church was to stand firm in the north of England for another 100 years.

In 626 Ethelbert's daughter, Ethelburga, married the pagan King Edwin, who had taken the throne of Northumbria ten years earlier by killing his rival, King Ethelfrith (see page 19).

The Archbishop of Canterbury took the opportunity to send with Ethelburga the monk Paulinus to convert the north to the Roman rites and to be the first Archbishop of York.

Paulinus' mission came to an abrupt end in 633 with the death of King Edwin at the hands of the pagan King Penda of Mercia. Paulinus beat a hasty retreat to Kent, where he died in 644.

Meanwhile, the children of the late King Ethelfrith were living in exile in Scotland. One of them, Oswald, met some of the Celtic monks from Iona and converted to Christianity.

Fired with missionary zeal, Oswald ousted King Penda and claimed Northumbria for himself in 634. He chose the Celtic monk Aidan to be Archbishop of Northumbria. Aidan chose Lindisfarne as his base. Paulinus' church in **York** sat in limbo.

Thus the north of England followed the Celtic tradition which tended to the hermitage and individual prayer, while the south followed the Roman tradition with its extensive hierarchy, wealth and pomp.

King Penda of Mercia returned to kill Oswald in 641 but was killed in turn by Oswald's brother Oswy in 655.

In 657 a Celtic monk called Eata started to build an abbey in **Ripon** on land granted by King Oswy's son Alcfrith. A year later Alcfrith changed his mind and offered the abbacy to an aristocratic Benedictine monk called Wilfrid.

Although educated at Lindisfarne, Wilfrid travelled to Rome and converted to the Roman rites. When he returned to England he accepted Alcfrith's offer and built an imposing (for the time) stone church at the site of Ripon Cathedral. The modest wooden church of Eata was abandoned. Eata later became abbot of Lindisfarne and bishop of Hexham. He died in 686.

Women also joined the monastic movement and became powerful in their own right. One such was Hilda. She studied under Paulinus, became a Benedictine nun and rose to the position of abbess.

In 657 Hilda built a double monastery for monks and nuns at **Whitby**. Whitby Abbey soon gained a reputation for justice, devotion and chastity. When King Oswy assembled a council of bishops (or synod) to decide between the Roman and Celtic churches he chose Whitby Abbey to be the place where the course of Christianity in England would be determined.

Wilfrid was the prime supporter of the Roman rites at the Synod of Whitby and was instrumental in their imposition on the Celtic church of Northumbria. When

Oswy chose in favour of the Roman church (reluctantly one suspects), the Archbishop of Northumbria retired. His successor died of the plague. To reward Wilfrid for his support Theodore, the Archbishop of Canterbury, awarded him the position.

It seems the English bishops at the time had questionable credentials because Theodore sent Wilfrid to Gaul to be consecrated. On Wilfrid's return he found that his patron Alcfrith, King Oswy's troublesome son, had inconveniently died and that Oswy had appointed Chad, a supporter of the Celtic rites, bishop of Northumbria with his seat at York.

Theodore removed Chad, on the grounds that he had been consecrated by the questionable bishops, but soon recognised his worth and made him bishop of Mercia. Wilfrid took up his Episcopal throne in York in 669.

King Oswy died in 670. The new king, Egfrith, favoured Wilfrid, who built new minsters at Ripon and Hexham (see Tour 4) and improved the cathedral at York. However, Wilfrid went a bit too far by encouraging Egfrith's wife Etheldreda to desert her husband to become a nun.

Wilfrid's wealth and power were beginning to worry Theodore 56

too, so he split Northumbria into four sees (areas under the ecclesiastical authority of a bishop or archbishop).

Wilfrid travelled to Rome to complain to the pope, who decided in his favour. On his return to England Egfrith imprisoned him, then exiled him to East Anglia.

When Egfrith died in 686, Aldfrith, his successor, allowed Wilfrid to return – but Wilfrid, obviously a slow learner, pushed Aldfrith too far and Theodore made him resign the bishopric of York in 691. Wilfrid appealed to the pope who again settled in his favour, but this time Wilfrid agreed to accept the sees of Hexham and Ripon.

Wilfrid died in 709 and was buried in the crypt under the high altar at Ripon.

Thus, the struggle for power between the Roman pope and the kings of England began centuries before Henry VIII ran into his difficulties.

Towards the end of the eighth century England came under attack by the Vikings, who rampaged, pillaged and eventually settled in the north of England in the area known as Danelaw. Many monasteries were destroyed and the monks killed.

The Norman Conquest

In 1066 King Harold had just repelled the last Viking attack in the north when William, who was just one step removed from being a Viking (or "norse man") himself, landed in the south. He conquered the south in one battle. Subduing the north took three attempts and the devastation of Northumbria.

The lands of the dead or dispossessed Anglo-Saxons were redistributed to Norman lords, who were strong supporters of religious houses: after all, someone has to pray for your soul if you leave death and destruction in your wake. Existing abbeys were restored and new ones founded.

The Black Death of 1348-49 had a dramatic effect on the rural economy. The few surviving labourers demanded higher wages and. landless peasants became tenant farmers.

The monastic orders shrank then regrouped. Affairs gradually improved over the next 100 or so years and abbots became powerful once again. Too powerful for their own good.

Dissolution

Henry VIII sought papal approval for his marriage to Anne Boleyn following his divorce of Catherine of Aragon. The pope refused and

Norman soldiers march north
©Regia Anglorum

in 1531 Henry declared himself head of the church in England.

The allegiance of the wealthy and powerful abbots was to the pope rather than to Henry. Henry was short of cash at the time and realised that he could eliminate his financial worries and the troublesome abbots by dissolving (destroying) the monasteries. He began in 1536 and in four years all were gone.

Most were sold to private individuals. Roofs were removed to expedite ruination and the stones were incorporated into manor houses. By the mid-eighteenth century many, such as Fountains, had become highly desirable romantic ruins in fashionable gardens.

York

Mainline rail station: YORK

There is so much to see and do in this lovely city that you will want to stay at least a couple of days. It is a convenient place from which to visit Castle Howard and Selby Abbey. The TIC, where you can pick up a city map, is conveniently located in the rail station.

The City

York was settled over 2,000 years ago. Its defensive walls enclose a roughly triangular area of streets laid out apparently at random. No doubt it all made sense at the time but the dearth of street signs makes finding your way very frustrating.

Help is at hand: the Association of Voluntary Guides to the City of York provides a free two-hour walk that starts outside the City Art Gallery in Exhibition Square daily at 10.15 and 14.15. In June, July and August a third tour starts at 18.45. Advance reservations are not necessary: just wait by the sign near the bus stops in front of the Art Gallery.

For a walk focussed on a specific topic, try Yorkwalk.

Yorkwalk
Cost: A £5.00/Co,YHA £4.50/ Ch£2.00
Tel. 01904 622 303
W: www.yorkwalk.co.uk

Yorkwalk leads special interest walks covering everything from Graveyards, Coffins & Plagues to Choccies & Sweeties.

York Minster
Open Mo-Sa 9.00-18.00
Su 12.00-18.00
Cost:
Minster A £5.00/Co £3.50/Ch free
Undercroft, Treasury & Crypt
A £3.50/Co £3.00/Ch £2.00
Combined A £7.00/Co £5.00
Tel. 01904 557 216
W: www.yorkminster.org

York Minster is a record-holder in several categories: it is the largest gothic cathedral north of the Alps, has the largest medieval stained-glass window in the world (the east window, created by master glazier John Thornton between 1405 and 1408) and the largest collection of stained glass in Britain.

There has been a church of some sort on the site for almost 1,400 years. The first was most likely that of Paulinus, the monk who arrived in the north with Ethelburga in 627.

St. Cuthbert was consecrated bishop here in 685. The St. Cuthbert window, on the south side of the choir, depicts incidents from his life. For more on Cuthbert, see page 20.

Fires, Vikings and time destroyed the early incarnations of the Minster. Of the present building the south transept dates from 1220; the north transept from 1260; the chapter house, 1300; the nave, 1338; the choir, 1450; the western towers, 1472; and the central tower, 1480. The minster thus offers examples of the three Gothic phases of English architecture: Early English (c. 1190–1300), Decorated (c. 1250–1380) and Perpendicular (c. 1350–1550).

Everyone is welcome to the services, which are held in the choir, and a useful little instructional leaflet is provided for those unfamiliar with the rites. Entrance for a service is free.

Treasurer's House (NT)
Open Mo-Sa 11.00-16.30
Cost: House A £4.80/Ch £2.40
House and cellar A £6.80/Ch
£3.60. NT members pay £2.00 for cellar tour
Tel. 01904 624 247
E: treasurershouse
@nationaltrust.org.uk

In 1897 a Yorkshire industrialist called Frank Green bought the early 17thC buildings that had been built on the site of the medieval house of York Minster's treasurers. The buildings were restored by architect Temple Moore, and over the next 33 years Green lovingly transformed the house into a showpiece for his collection of antique furniture.

Knowledgeable National Trust room stewards will be delighted to answer your questions.

The house stands on what was the Via Decumana, the principal road through Eboracum, as York was called by the Romans. Therein lies the tale of the Forgotten Army, a Roman regiment from AD390.

This eerie and moving story is related in situ during the tour of the cellar. Entry to this small enclosed space is by timed ticket. Hard hats are provided and must be worn.

GOOD EATING
The Treasurer's House licensed tea room serves light meals and snacks based on traditional Yorkshire recipes.

Merchant Adventurers' Hall
Open Mo-Th 9.00-17.00
Fr-Sa 9.00-15.30; Su 12.00-16.00
Cost: A £2.50/Co £2.00/Ch £1.00
Tel. 01904 654 818
W: www.theyorkcompany.co.uk

Built between 1357 and 1361, the Ancient Guild Hall of the Company of Merchant Adventurers of the City of York was the first guild hall to be built in Britain. The guild, or association, met to discuss business in the Great Hall, while its religious and charitable obligations were fulfilled by a chapel and a hospital for the poor.

Of particular interest is the fascinating arrangement of beams supporting the roof of the Great Hall. In the Undercroft hang twenty banners depicting the coats of arms of various medieval guilds. Try matching the trade to the banner using the tools depicted on each as clues.

The admission charge includes an excellent audio tour. The Hall sits in a very lovely garden, which is not exactly peaceful, since it is beside a busy shopping street, but is a pleasant place to sit for a while.

Jorvik Viking Centre
Open daily 10.00-17.00
Cost: A £7.45/Co £6.30/Ch £5.25
Reduced joint ticket for Dig! and Jorvik Viking Centre. EH members 15% discount, YHA discount. Pre-book tickets to bypass the queue by telephone or online.
Tel. 01904 543 403
W: www.vikingjorvik.com

This popular attraction starts with a journey back in time to the reconstructed town of Jorvik, complete with the sights, sounds and

York Minster

smells you might expect from a 1,000-year old Viking settlement.

There follows an exhibition of artefacts found on the site.

The queue to enter the Jorvik Viking Centre has become a York feature in itself. You can avoid the wait by pre-booking your tickets by telephone or online.

Dig!

Open daily 10.00-17.00
Cost: A £4.50/CoCh £4.00
Reduced joint ticket for Dig! and Jorvik Viking Centre. EH members 15% discount.
Tel. 01904 543 403
W: www.digyork.com

Dig! is a new attraction opening April 2006. Visitors work in a simulated excavation to find real artefacts from York's Roman, Viking, Medieval and Victorian past. The "discovered" items will be examined in a fieldwork tent, a laboratory and a researchers' library. Visitors analyse their finds using the latest technology.

Castle Museum of Daily Life

Open daily 9.30-17.00
Cost: A £6.50/Co £5.00/Ch £3.50
Tel. 01904 687 687
W: www.york.castle.museum

Fascinating and fun for all ages. Six hundred years of everyday life, with a cobbled Victorian street and the prison cell that housed Dick Turpin. You might find something

from your own house in there!

Clifford's Tower (EH)

Open daily Apr-Sep 10.00-18.00
Oct 10.00-17.00
Cost: A £2.80/Co £2.10/Ch £1.40
Tel. 01904 646 940

To maintain his hold on the rebellious north, William the Conqueror built many strategically located motte and bailey forts. A motte is an artificial mound surrounded by a ditch. A bailey is the area within fortified walls. The original baileys consisted of a palisade around a wooden tower on top of the motte. This arrangement was quick to build and easy to defend. Later, the wooden structures were replaced by stone and the bailey expanded to include an area around the motte.

Clifford's Tower is fine example of a later motte and bailey castle. The stone tower was built by Henry III in the thirteenth century.

Norman knight
©Regia Anglorum

It was officially called the King's Tower until 1596 when the first reference to Clifford's Tower appears. The body of one Sir Roger Clifford had hung from chains in the tower after his defeat at the battle of Boroughbridge in 1322. This appears to be the only Clifford connection to the tower.

Clifford's Tower has survived flood, fire, sabotage and subsidence. Now it stands stolidly against the serried ranks of cars in the surrounding car park.

On the whole, Clifford's Tower is more impressive from the outside than the inside; however, it is good fun to climb the worn spiral staircase and walk the walls, which give good views over York.

Access to the interior is up a long flight of steep steps.

Yorkshire Museum
Open daily 10.00-17.00
Cost: £4.00/Co £3.00/Ch £2.50
Tel. 01904 687 687
W: www.york.yorkshire.museum

The Roman and Viking sections are very text-heavy. The medieval and prehistoric displays are visually more exciting and include the remains of the Chapter House of St. Mary's Abbey, whence thirteen disgruntled Benedictine monks set out to found Fountains Abbey.

Pride of place is the 15thC gold and sapphire jewel found near Middleham castle, the preferred home of the much maligned King Richard III.

The museum is surrounded by ten acres of botanical gardens that are gradually absorbing the ruins of St. Mary's Abbey, a 14thC Hospitium and a section of York's Roman fortress.

National Railway Museum
Open daily 10.00-18.00
Cost: free
Tel. 01904 621 261
W: www.nrm.org.uk

This, the world's largest railway museum, displays examples of engines and carriages spanning the history of rail travel.

The collection of Royal Trains, together with disembodied voices recounting memories of Royal encounters, is fascinating.

There is a model railway to observe, a miniature railway to ride, turntable demonstrations and The Works and Warehouse.

With indoor and outdoor picnic areas and several cafes, this could be a day trip for the real enthusiast or take an hour or so for the merely curious. There is probably something of interest here for everyone. Children under thirteen must be supervised at all times: the museum is huge!

Pay full price at any one museum marked thus ❀ then pay half price at the others so marked.

⊕ Richard III Museum

Open daily 9.00-17.00
Cost: A £2.50/Co £1.25/Ch free
Tel. 01904 634 191
W: www.richardiiimuseum.co.uk

This small, slightly amateurish museum is located in Monk Bar, a fourteenth century guard house incorporated into a city gate or "bar". In 1484 Richard III ordered and paid for the building of the room that now houses most of the display.

Access from street level is by a flight of steep, dark stairs inside the Bar. Using an audio "trial" and mock newspaper reports, the controversy over who murdered King Richard's nephews in the Tower of London (a royal residence) is explained. Was it Richard III, as the Tudor propagandists would have it, or Henry VII, who had a much stronger motive, or…? After listening to the trial and reading the "reports" you are invited to reach your own verdict.

The study of Richard III is highly addictive! At the very least, his story should cause you to question every bit of history you were ever taught. To learn more read Josephine Tey's *The Daughter of Time* and proceed from there.

With the Little Ease prison room, the garderobe (medieval toilet) and the executioner's block and axe, the building itself is worth a visit and is more atmospheric than Clifford's Tower.

From Monk Bar walk along the wall to Bootham Bar. This stretch provides the best views of the Minster and into gardens and houses.

⊕ Eboracum Legion Bathhouse

Open Mo-Fr 10.00-17.00
Sa-Su 10.00-16.00
Cost: A £2.00/Co £1.50/Ch £1.00
Tel. 01904 620 455

This unpolished not-quite gem is a partially excavated Roman bathhouse with full-size models to provide atmosphere. Drop by if you have never seen a Roman bathhouse. Children will enjoy it.

⊕ Barley Hall Medieval Townhouse

Open Tu-Su/BH 10.00-16.00
Cost: A£3.50/Co 2.50/Ch £2.50
Tel. 01904 610 275
W: www.barleyhall.org.uk

A work-in-progress, this site is being extensively renovated. It will eventually be a "working, living" medieval house. There are lots of activities for children and much of interest for adults. The audio tour is painfully long and unbelievably tedious in places but does have a few interesting bits.

BASE: YORK

Half-Day Trip to Castle Howard

A very pretty one-hour bus journey ends about one and a half miles from this ornate stately home with lovely woods, formal gardens and landscaped grounds. The bus service allows a visit of about three and a half hours: sufficient for a tour of the house and relaxed stroll through most of the grounds. Allow about 30 minutes to walk from the Stable Courtyard to the bus stop. For a more in-depth exploration of the woods and time for lunch, return by the later bus.

GETTING THERE
Bus 181 d. York (Piccadilly) Mo-Sa about 8.30 and 11.00 (1 hour) No Su service. Ask driver for Castle Howard (crossroads near We-burn). The castle is 1½ miles from the bus stop straight up the road with the big stone arch (30 min walk uphill).

Return 13.00 and 15.30. The stop is on the right hand corner of the crossroads as you return from the castle. Do not cross the road.

OR last week of May-Sep Bus 840 d. York rail stn for Castle Howard (5 min walk from castle) Mo-Su once in the morning and returns once in the afternoon (38 min)

Castle Howard
Open House daily 11.00. Last admission 16.00
Gardens and Park daily 10.00-18.30 Last admission 16.00

Stately peacock near the Atlas Fountain at Castle Howard
by kind permission of Castle Howard Estate Ltd.

Arboretum. Tu-Su/BH 10.00-18.00
Cost: House and Grounds A £9.50
Co £8.50/Ch £6.50
Grounds A £6.50/Co £6.00/Ch
£4.50
Arboretum: A £4.00/Ch £2.00
EH members discount on combined house and garden ticket.
Tel. 01653 648 333
W: www.castlehoward.co.uk

Howards have lived at the Castle for over 300 years. It is still very much their home in spite of being run as a business. Of course, great estates probably always had to be successful businesses in order to survive.

Take the first bus of the day from York to arrive at the entrance as the grounds open. Allow an hour for the house.

As you walk from the Stable Courtyard to the house, look out for a modest door in the wall on the right. It opens into a walled garden that leads to the rose garden. Both are secluded and serene – if you arrive before the crowds.

Mind the peacocks around the Atlas Fountain, then stroll beside the lakes to the Temple of the Four Winds and the view of the Cascade, Mausoleum and New River Bridge. Return to the castle by Ray Wood. This is planted with daffodils, rhododendron and exotic plants, such as bamboo, that thrive in the microclimate of the Wood. Back by the castle don't miss the very smug boar presiding over his own garden!

Friendly room stewards offer detailed information on the furniture and paintings, as well as stories from the past. Ask about the fire started by the girls of Queen Margaret's School in 1940.

Within the Stable Courtyard is a farm shop selling estate and local produce, a chocolate shop, gift shop, glass studio and bookshop.

Finally, there is a 150-acre Arboretum – a collaboration between the Royal Botanic Gardens at Kew and the Castle Howard Estate. Here you will see rare plants and trees, as well as a variety of birds and wild flowers.

GOOD EATING

The *Courtyard Café* and the *Fitzroy Room* serve meals prepared using estate or locally produced ingredients. Expect to pay at least £8.00 for a main course. The *Lakeside Café* serves ice cream, drinks and pizzas from 11.30 – 14.30 Sa, Su, BH and school holidays

BASE: YORK

Half-Day Trip to Selby Abbey

Selby is a dull 45-minute bus trip from York. The reason for the visit is Selby Abbey, considered to be one of the three great churches in Yorkshire (the others being York Minster and Beverley Minster). If you are at all interested in ecclesiastic architecture and especially if you cannot visit Durham Cathedral, then a trip to Selby Abbey is worth the effort.

> **GETTING to SELBY**
> Buses 412, 413, 415 d. Piccadilly (opposite the Merchant Adventurers' Hall) for Selby bus stn Mo-Sa 3/hr; Su 1-2/hr (45 min). Selby Abbey is adjacent to Selby market place, in sight of the bus station.

Selby Abbey
Open daily Apr-Sep 9.00-17.00
Oct 9.00-16.00
Cost: free
W: www.selbyabbey.co.uk

Selby was the first monastery to be founded in the north of England after the Norman Conquest.

In 1069 a Benedictine monk called Benedict (not the saint) arrived from France with a dried finger of St. Germain. In thanksgiving for his victory over the north William the Conqueror granted Benedict a charter to found a monastery in Selby.

Benedict built a wooden church but was obliged to resign his abbacy after castrating two of his monks. They had left the monastery and taken some of its treasures with them.

Benedict's successor began building a stone church, much of which stands today. Unfortunately the foundations were on unstable ground, so as the tower grew it also sank. The tower eventually stabilised, but look for the distorted arches at its base.

It took about 130 years to complete the building, which thus spans the Norman and early English architectural periods. The interior is quite a contrast to the Decorated and Perpendicular York Minster!

When Henry VIII dissolved the monasteries in 1539 the abbey buildings were destroyed, but the church remained. In 1618 it was officially designated the parish church.

The church had its troubles: it was used as barracks and stables during the Civil War in 1643, the tower collapsed in 1690 and the nave burned in 1906. Each time it was cleaned and repaired and today is still an active parish church.

Day 1 – York to Ripon

North of the soft rolling fields around York the ground becomes hillier and the houses stonier. Ripon could hardly be described as rugged, but you may begin to feel that you are within reach of the true north country.

Ripon's vicarious claim to fame is being the town closest to the World Heritage Site of Fountains Abbey and Studley Royal; however, it would be wrong to dismiss it as just another pleasant Yorkshire market town. It has an outstanding feature of its own – Ripon Cathedral.

GETTING to RIPON
Bus 142,146 d. Piccadilly for Ripon bus stn Mo-Sa 1/hr (80 minutes). The bus station is about 5 minutes' walk from the market square (see map). No Su service.

Ripon cathedral
Open from 10.00
Cost: free

With the internment of the argumentative monk Wilfrid (see page 55) in the crypt beneath the high altar in 709, Ripon Cathedral became a focus for pilgrims.

In 948 the cathedral was damaged by fire, not by Vikings, the usual culprits at the time, but by the English King Eadred, because Northumbria had accepted Viking rule.

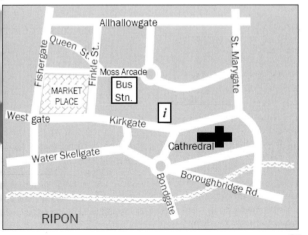

The body of St. Cuthbert and various bits of St. Oswald rested here for a while in 995 before settling in Durham. For more on St. Oswald see page 19.

A new building, with a shrine to St. Wilfrid, was built in the twelfth century. The shrine was destroyed at the orders of the commissioners of Henry VIII in 1539, but the building itself survived as a parish church.

The diocese of Ripon was recreated in 1836, and the church became, once again, a cathedral. In 2000 the diocese expanded and Ripon is now the seat of the bishop of Leeds and Ripon.

All that remains of the original building is the 7[th]C crypt, which is open to the public. It was vandalised in 2005, so entry may now be restricted.

The church has been continually expanded, repaired and renovated. Twentieth century figures fill the niches of the 15[th]C stone pulpitum that separates the choir from the nave, medieval wall paintings decorate the chapels on the east side of the transepts, there is an Arts & Crafts movement pulpit, some vicious-looking 20[th]C ironwork guarding the Chapel of the Holy Spirit and statuary spanning the entire 800 years of the building's existence.

The transepts show the 12[th]C transition from the rounded Norman style to the pointed Early

This type of decoration is typical of Norman arches and doorways.
The west front of Selby Abbey.

English style. The west front is Early English, while the choir, built about 100 years later, is Decorated.

The tower collapsed in 1450 and was rebuilt, together with the nave, in the Perpendicular style. The central tower now stands on two pointed Perpendicular arches and two rounded Transitional arches.

A free leaflet provides a brief tour of the cathedral and a volunteer in a blue robe wanders around the interior answering questions.

Look for the 17thC mechanical hand that the organist used to direct the choir whilst he remained seated in the organ loft.

Also in the choir is a possible link to Lewis Carol and Alice in Wonderland. One of the misericords shows a griffin chasing a rabbit down a hole.

Two nights in Ripon

Day 2 – Fountains Abbey & Studley Royal

Fountains Abbey and Studley Royal Water Garden (EH & NT)
Open daily
Abbey, mill & garden 10.00-17.00
Shop & Restaurant 10.00-18.00
St. Mary's Apr-Sep 13.00-17.00
Cost: Abbey & garden A £5.50/ Ch £3.00
Deer park and St. Mary's free
Tel. 01765 608 888
E: fountainsenquiries
@nationaltrust.org.uk

GETTING THERE
Bus 139 d. Ripon bus stn for Fountains Visitor Centre Mo-Sa & BH 3/day (20 min). Return buses allow about 3½-5 hours at Fountains. Bus also stops at Fountains Abbey Deer Park. No Su service.

In the eighteenth century a picturesque ruin was the finishing touch to a modish garden: "I've got a Cistercian abbey in mine. What do you have in yours?" sort of thing.

This World Heritage Site features a 12thC Cistercian abbey and watermill, a medieval deer park with red, fallow and sika deer, an Elizabethan mansion, a Georgian water garden and an ornate Victorian Gothic church. Improve on that if you can!

Fountains Abbey

Following a monastic riot at St. Mary's Abbey in York, Archbishop Thurstan removed thirteen discontented monks to his palace at Ripon. On 27 December 1132 these monks walked the three miles to the land Thurstan had granted them in order to build a new abbey – Fountains – that would strictly follow the Rule of St. Benedict.

69

In spite of their best efforts they could not survive alone. Since the well-established Cistercian order had been founded on the same principles as Fountains the monks turned to them for help. Fountains became a Cistercian abbey in 1135.

With the help of wealthy donors, the business skills of the choir monks and the physical labour of the lay brothers, Fountains Abbey grew into a powerful organisation with substantial agricultural and industrial interests.

What followed was common to most monasteries of the time: rapid growth and over-expansion followed by economic collapse assisted by Scottish raids, poor harvests and the plague.

In 1536 Marmaduke Bradley, a Cistercian monk and a canon of Ripon, successfully bribed the king's secretary, Thomas Cromwell, with his prebend (the canonical house in Ripon) and £200 in exchange for the abbacy of Fountains. When Henry VIII dissolved the monastery three years later Bradley co-operated and was rewarded with an annual pension of £100. He retired to his prebend, which Cromwell never received, and lived in comfort until his death in 1553.

The abbey buildings and 500 acres of surrounding land were sold. Stones from the abbey were used to build a manor, Fountains Hall, close to the abbey gatehouse. Two rooms of this Elizabethan home are open to the public.

Studley Royal

The grounds of Studley Royal are a spectacular example of 18thC landscape design: a fusion of picturesque and formal. They are the life work of John Aislabie and his son William.

John inherited the property (excluding the abbey and Fountains Hall) in 1699. He first laid out the water garden in the valley, building a canal to divert the river and create cascades, ponds and a lake. Trees and shrubs were planted to form scenic vistas that would reveal themselves unexpectedly to the walker in the garden.

He then built the follies that abound in the woods, slopes and valley. There is a Greek temple, an octagonal tower, a rotunda and a small banqueting house, as well as classical statues, all strategically located to provide unforgettable views.

John Aislabie died in 1742, but his son William continued the work. In 1768 William bought Fountains Abbey and Fountains Hall. The abbey became the highlight of the gardens. There is even a special structure, Anne Boleyn's Seat, situated to provide the best view. Ironic really, since the fall of the abbey was an indirect result of Henry VIII's desire to marry Anne Boleyn, whom he subsequently beheaded.

The Aislabie manor house at Studley Royal was destroyed by fire in 1946 and the site cleared.

Fountains was acquired by the National Trust in 1983.

St. Mary's Church

The Church of St. Mary the Virgin was built for the first Marquess and Marchioness of Ripon. The interior is extravagantly Victorian Gothic, with extensive use of marble and gilded woodwork. The effect is rich and glows in the light that streams through the stained glass windows intensifying the colours within.

Day 3 – Ripon to Thirsk to Osmotherley

Thirsk was the home of the man behind James Herriot, the vet featured in a collection of books and on a television series. The surgery, "Skeldale House", is open to the public.

Osmotherley is a little village not far from the Carthusian Mount Grace Priory.

No Sunday public transport service to Osmotherley. Overnight in Osmotherley.

Thirsk

This pleasant market town is quietly proud of its James Herriot connection. Certainly everyone can point you in the right direction for the World of James Herriot, located at 23 Kirkgate, less than five minutes' walk from the bus stop at the market square.

GETTING THERE
Bus 70 d. Ripon for Thirsk Mo-Sa every 2 hr (40 min). If you do not want to visit the World of James Herriot, stay on the bus and continue to Northallerton for the connection to Osmotherley.

World of James Herriot

Open daily Easter-Oct 10.00–18.00; Nov-Easter 11.00-16.00
Cost: A £4.95/Co £3.90/Ch £3.40
Tel. 01845 524 234
W: www.worldofjamesherriot.org

This fascinating and atmospheric museum is within the original "Skeldale House". The rooms are arranged as they were in the 1940s and are peopled with some unnervingly realistic models. You will learn about the life and times of the real vet, author Alf Wight, as well as the making of the television series.

This is the only museum in the U.K. dedicated to veterinary science: past and present. There is a lot to see and enjoy. The learning room will spark interest in adults as well as the intended children!

GOOD EATING in THIRSK

The Upstairs Downstairs Tea Room, located on the right hand corner of Kirkgate as you return to the square, provides light lunches and teas in a traditional surrounding. The service is offhand but the food is tasty.

There are pubs and bakeries in Thirsk and in Northallerton, where you change bus for Osmotherley, so you have several eating options.

Thirsk to Osmotherley

GETTING THERE
Bus 70 d. Thirsk for Northallerton Buck Inn Mo-Sa every 2 hr (25 min)
Bus 80/89 d. Northallerton Buck Inn for Osmotherley Mo-Sa 1/hr (20 min)

Osmotherley is a small village encircling a market cross and miniature green. The bus stops in the centre of the village very close to the Queen Catherine Hotel. A walking supplies shop, where you can get advice on visiting Mount Grace Priory, is opposite the Hotel.

GOOD EATING

The restaurant of the *Queen Catherine Hotel* offers a range of traditional English meals at a not-too-expensive price. Although the restaurant is a no-smoking area, some smoke does drift over from the bar.

The Carthusians in England

The Carthusians arrived in England in 1178 at the invitation of Henry II (whose hasty words led to the killing of Thomas Becket). The first charterhouses, as they were called, were in the south.

The movement grew slowly at first, but the Black Death of 1348–49, which ravaged other religious orders, encouraged people to support the Carthusians, who, being isolated, were minimally affected. The order expanded northwards.

Mount Grace Priory (NT & EH)

Tel. 01609 883 494
Open Apr-Sep daily 10.00-18.00
Oct Th-Mo 10.00-16.00
Cost: A £3.60/Co £2.70/Ch £1.80
Tel. 01609 883 494

GETTING THERE
BY BUS
Bus 80/89 (the same one you arrived on) continues to Stokesley with a stop at Priory Road End. From there it is a flat ½ mile walk (5-10 min)

OR BY FOOT
About 2 miles, some hills, one of

them steep.

Turn left at the T-junction in the village centre into North End. Walk up the hill and in about ¼ mile turn left into Ruebury Lane. A path that branches off to the right goes uphill to a Lady Chapel. Continue on the lane until you reach a farm on your left. The Cleveland Way continues straight ahead, but you need to go down into the farmyard.

You will see some fields sloping downhill to some woods. Go through the gate into the left-most of these fields and walk straight downhill to the next gate. Go through, turn left and follow the wall along two sides of the field until you reach the bottom, where a stile crosses a wall into the wood in front of you.

The path goes steeply downhill and is slippery when wet. Look out for pheasants, rabbits and ducks. The steep bit isn't too long and the return journey is manageable for any one who is sound in wind and limb.

The path will eventually take you to a stile into a field. Continue over the stile and turn right. The gate to the lane leading to Mount Grace Priory is about 100 yards ahead.

Mount Grace Priory was founded in 1398 by Thomas de Holland, Duke of Surrey and nephew of Richard II. He chose Bordelbi, an estate that he leased from the king and that he had, in turn, leased to John de Ingleby, who had lived there with his family for 36 years.

Richard II was deposed in 1399

Mount Grace Priory

73

and Thomas de Holland was executed. Henry IV continued to provide an annual grant to Mount Grace and, since the de Hollands had not been dispossessed, Thomas's brother continued as patron to the priory.

By 1438 the advowson (the right to bestow land on a religious order) of Bordelbi had passed to the Ingleby family. They wanted their home back, but the Carthusians were ahead of them on that: they had had their title to the land confirmed. Ingleby wasn't ready to give up and gave the manor and estate to the Augustinians at Gisborough Priory. However, the Augustinians agreed to lease the land to the Carthusians for £8.00 a year.

Mount Grace underwent the usual fluctuations of fortune and was thriving when Prior Wilson was obliged to surrender it to King Henry VIII in 1539.

The property was then purchased from the crown for the sake of the land; the buildings were left to decay. The priory guest house was eventually converted into a manor, which was subsequently rebuilt in 1898. At about the same time excavation and repair began on the remains of the priory buildings and have continued to the present. The site was given to the government in lieu of death duties in 1953.

Mount Grace illustrates the standard arrangement of a Carthusian monastery. The Great Cloister garth is surrounded by the "cells" of the monks. One of these has been reconstructed, and you will see that it really is a very snug bijou residence.

The priory church is small and simple compared to the abbey churches of the Benedictines and Cistercians because the Carthusian monks' lives were centred about private prayer rather than communal services.

The whole place is very peaceful if visited out of peak hours and, combined with the walk from Osmotherley, makes for a very pleasant late afternoon outing.

Day 4 – Osmotherley to Ormesby Hall to Whitby

From Osmotherley the route continues to Whitby with an optional side trip en route to the Palladian Ormesby Hall. The Hall is not spectacular but is attractive in a modest way and is of considerable architectural interest. Unfortunately, although the gates to the property are directly opposite the bus stop it is a good 20 to 25 minutes' walk, with your bags, to reach the Hall itself, so unless Palladian architecture is of particular interest to you, giving it a miss is a reasonable option.

There is no Sunday bus service from Osmotherley and **Ormesby Hall is only open Friday to Monday**. Two nights in Whitby.

GETTING to WHITBY
direct from OSMOTHERLEY
Bus 80,89 d. Osmotherley (The Cross) for Stokesley High St. Mo-Sa 1/hr (35 min). No Su service.

Bus 90,29 d. Stokesley High St for Middlesborough bus stn Mo-Sa 3/hr; Su 1/hr (50 min).

Bus X56 departs Middlesborough bus stn for Whitby bus stn Mo-Sa 2/hr until 16.15 then 1/hr; Su 1/hr (1½ hr)
OR Bus 93 d. Middlesborough bus stn for Whitby Mo-Sa 1/hr a.m. and evening; Su 2/day (70 min)
This last leg, though lengthy, is very attractive, running through the North Yorkshire Moors to the coast. *Motion Sickness Alert!*

Ormesby Hall (NT)
Open House Fr-Mo 13.30-17.00
Shop/tea room Fr-Mo 12.30-17.00
Cost: A£4.10/Ch £2.00
Tel. 01642 324 188
E: ormesbyhall@nationaltrust.org.uk

GETTING to ORMESBY HALL
It takes a bit over an hour to get from Osmotherley to the gates of Ormesby Hall. Time your departure to arrive in time for lunch. Bus 80,89 as above to Stokesley High St, then Bus 90, 29 as above, but ask for Marton crossroads, on the outskirts of Middlesbrough (25 min).

There is a bus stop on the left corner on Ladgate Lane (see map) where you can pick up Bus 63 (Mo-Sa 6/hr, Su 2/hr) and ask to be dropped off for Ormesby Hall (5 min). Cross the road, pro-

MIDDLESBOROUGH

MARTON
CROSSROADS

Ladgate Lane
To Ormesby Hall

X = Bus stop for
Ormesby Hall
● = Get off here

STOKESLEY

ceed through the gates and follow the lane to the house, keeping to the left whenever it branches (25 min walk).

You can also walk from Marton crossroads along Ladgate Lane until you reach the gates, but the whole walk is quite long, especially with luggage.

Ormesby Hall is a Palladian house that started quite small but grew with the family fortunes. The plasterwork of the ceilings is particularly fine. The paintings range from 18thC portraits to highly meaningful pieces from the 1980s. Below stairs is a large kitchen and scullery.

The room stewards are enthusiastic raconteurs well up on the family background and the contents of the rooms.

Members of a model railway club use some of the upstairs rooms to lay out their tracks. Visitors are welcome.

The grounds are attractively laid out with the formal gardens melding into the surrounding park, somewhat like Fountains, but nowhere near as grand!

The stable block is let to the Cleveland Mounted Police, who may allow a visit, depending on the circumstances. Unfortunately,

there is no way to plan this one ahead of time, so it is a toss-up whether you see the stables or not.

Proceed to Whitby.

GETTING to WHITBY
from ORMESBY HALL
Return to the bus stop on the far side of the road from the gates to Ormesby Hall. Take Bus 63 and ask for Ormesby crossroads (5 min). Ask the driver to point out the bus stop for Whitby. It is located on the far side of the road from the post office.
OR
WALK to Ormesby crossroads by continuing along Ladgate Lane to the roundabout, turn left and cross the road to the bus stop (about 25 min).
Bus X56 departs Ormesby crossroads for Whitby bus stn Mo-Sa 2/hr until 16.15 then 1/hr; Su 1/hr (1 hr 20 min)
OR Bus 93 d. Ormesby crossroads for Whitby Mo-Sa 1/hr a.m. and evening; Su 2/day. (1hr)

This last leg, though lengthy, is very attractive, running through the North Yorkshire Moors to the coast. *Motion Sickness Alert!*

Both the bus station and the railway station at Whitby are within sight of the TIC where you can get a map and directions.

Day 5 – Whitby

Whitby retains its dignity as an active fishing port in spite of its increasing popularity as a tourist destination. Book your accommodation early, especially during school and bank holidays.

In addition to the famous Synod in 664, Whitby is associated with Captain James Cook, black jet jewellery and vampires.

This charismatic yet sturdy town is built on steep slopes on both sides of the River Esk. The older part is at the foot of the east cliff. Here are the shops selling jet, the Captain Cook Museum and the 199 stone steps leading up the cliff to St. Mary's Parish Church and Whitby Abbey.

The west cliff was developed in the eighteenth and nineteenth centuries. Most of the guest houses are located on this side in the former homes of wealthy seafarers and merchants. From the promenade by the Captain Cook Monument you can see the Abbey and St. Mary's church with its army of gravestones spreading and spilling down the cliff to the old town and the sea. This is a particularly stunning sight at night when the Abbey is illuminated.

Captain Cook sailed from Whitby and four of his ships were built here: *Endeavour, Resolution, Adventure* and *Discovery*. The town features in *Moby Dick, Sylvia's Lovers* and *Dracula*.

The beaches are sandy and the fish and chips are superb.

If you have the time for an extra day, you can either walk the six miles along the Cleveland Way or take a bus to Robin Hood's Bay – a tiny, beautiful one-time smuggling village.

Whitby Abbey (EH)
Open Apr-Sep daily 10.00-18.00
Oct Th-Mo 10.00-17.00
Cost: A £4.00/Co £3.00/Ch £2.00
Tel. 01947 603 568

Founded by the Benedictine abbess Hilda in 657, the abbey was chosen by King Oswy for the Synod of Whitby in 664.

When King Oswy defeated King Penda in 655 he gave his daughter, Elfleda, to the church. She was cared for and educated by Hilda and became a nun at Whitby.

On the death of King Oswy in 670 his widow, Enfleda, also entered Whitby as a nun and succeeded Hilda as abbess in 680. She, in turn, was succeeded by her daughter, Elfleda. It was Elfleda who persuaded the troublesome Wilfrid to stop arguing and accept the Sees of Hexham and Ripon in 705.

Hilda, Enfleda, Elfleda and Wilfrid were all sainted

Whitby Abbey maintained a worthy reputation, although it seems discipline gradually lapsed. Excavations in what is thought to have been the nuns' quarters have revealed jewellery, coins, silver and bronze ornaments and other more prosaic, but equally personal, items such as cooking pots and bowls. This private ownership was forbidden by the Rule of St. Benedict. One trusts this moral decline commenced after the abbacies of the three saints.

The abbey was destroyed by Vikings in 867.

The Venerable Bede visited Whitby and wrote enthusiastically of its worthiness in his *Ecclesiastical History of the English People* (731). More than 300 years later, in 1073, a Norman monk called Reinfrid searched for the abbeys described by Bede in his *History*. After visiting Bede's abbey in Jarrow and another in Wearmouth, Reinfrid and his companions arrived at Whitby.

They found the remains of almost forty small oratories of the original abbey. Reinfrid, who had been one of William the Conqueror's knights before turning monk, razed these and constructed a monastery following the standard continental ecclesiastical plans of the time. Where Anglo-Saxon monasteries had several small churches or chapels, perhaps derived from the eremitic tradition of the Celtic church, the Normans went for size.

The new Whitby abbey had wealthy benefactors. It accumulated estates and grew in wealth through agriculture. One of the abbey's prime assets was its unusually large collection of associated saints and a macabre selection of their bones (although St. Hilda's finished up in Glastonbury).

Whitby abbey strictly maintained the Rule of St. Benedict; lax monks were sent there for moral rehabilitation. Nevertheless, financial difficulties, which began with the ambitious expansion of its church, continued sporadically.

The Black Death of 1349 wrought the usual pattern of a diminished labour force in a strong position to demand increased wages. Order and discipline at Whitby declined: it was feared that, if the Rule was enforced too strictly, numbers would diminish catastrophically.

The abbey surrendered to Henry VIII in December 1539.

The property was leased, then sold to Richard Cholmley, who hastened the decay of the buildings by using their material to build his own manor, now also in ruins.

St. Mary's Parish Church

Open May-Aug 10.00-17.00
Sep-Oct 10.00-15.00
Tel. 01947 606578

Climb the 199 steps up the east cliff from the old part of Whitby to visit this extraordinarily peculiar church close to the abbey.

Building of the present structure began at the start of the twelfth century to replace an older church damaged during William the Conqueror's northern rampage.

The plan of the church is unusual in that there are no aisles in the nave. The walls of the nave and chancel date from 1110; the tower from 1170, the north transept from 1225, the south transept from 1380 and the north extension from 1819.

While the basic structure, with its mix of progressive styles, is only slightly out of the ordinary, it is the contents that boggle the mind. Picture, if you can, a combination of theatre auditorium and cattle market, made by a ship builder and decorated by a pretentious and too-rich admirer of Victorian gothic. Throw in some leftover carousel parts, shake well and see what happens.

There is a particularly tacky early 17thC structure called The Cholmley Pew in honour of the then Lords of the Manor. It is supported by four white, twisted, queasy-making columns and very effectively hides the lovely arch into the chancel. There is a three-decker pulpit (floor level for the Parish Clerk, middle level for priest taking the service and top level for giving the sermon), complete with hearing trumpets leading to the pew of the early 19thC minister's wife.

The church now seats 1,500 and has been used for worship for nearly 900 years.

The tall sandstone cross by the side of the church is late nineteenth century. It honours St. Caedmon, a cowherd at the abbey in St. Hilda's time. He became a monk as an adult and wrote religious poetry and songs in the vernacular. Only nine lines of his work survive, recorded in Bede's *Ecclesiastical History*.

Captain Cook Memorial Museum

Open daily 9.45-17.00
Cost: A £3.00/Sr £2.50/Ch £2.00
Tel. 01947 601 900
W: www.cookmuseumwhitby.co.uk

The museum is located on Grape Lane on the east side of the harbour immediately to south of the bridge. Although the house is seventeenth century, it is furnished in the style of 1746, the time when James Cook was apprenticed to ship owner John Walker, whose home it was. It contains, amongst other memorabilia, paintings by artists who accompanied Cook on his voyages of discovery.

Whitby Museum & Art Gallery

Open Tu-Su/BH 9.30-16.30
Cost: A £3.00/Co £2.50/Ch £1.00
Tel. 01947 602 908
W: www.durain.demon.co.uk

Located in Pannett Park on the West Cliff, this museum contains many artefacts from the voyages of Captain Cook and an important collection of Jurassic reptile fossils. The art gallery displays many paintings depicting 19thC Whitby.

Robin Hood's Bay

It is very unlikely that Robin Hood had anything to do with this odd little village. It's original name was simply Bay. The steep main street plunges directly to the tiny harbour once used by fishermen and smugglers. There are tunnels with trapdoors opening into some of the houses, which are themselves so closely packed that goods could be passed from home to home without touching the ground!

GETTING to ROBIN HOOD'S BAY
Bus 93 d. Whitby bus stn for Robin Hood's Bay Mo-Sa 1/hr, Su every 1-2 hr (19 min)
OR
Walk the Cleveland Way, which follows the coastal cliffs for most of the six miles from Whitby.

Day 6 – Whitby to Helmsley

From Grosmont, near Whitby, a train runs through the north Yorkshire moors to Pickering. From there it is a 40-minute bus ride to Helmsley.

Pickering is an attractive town in its own right, and you may wish to explore it before continuing to Helmsley. Alternatively, take a side trip to Eden Camp, a prisoner of war camp converted into a fascinating war-time museum.

There is a great deal to see and do in Helmsley, and if you can only spare one night I recommend getting there as early as possible.

GETTING to PICKERING by TRAIN
Train d. Whitby for Grosmont Mo-Sa 4/day; Su last week of May to mid-Sep 5/day (17 min) Change at Grosmont for North Yorkshire Moors Railway (NYMR).
NYMR d. Grosmont for Pickering Mo-Su 1/hr (50 min) Connects with train from Whitby at 10.15 and 13.15. Some days special

times apply. Timetables are available from Whitby rail station and TIC or Tel. 01751 473535 or visit www.northyorkshiremoorsrailway.com

Goathland, the station after Grosmont, is known in the wizard world as Hogsmeade station.

GETTING from RAIL STATION to BUS STOP

From Pickering rail stn turn right into the road then turn left at the first intersection (the Market Place will be to your left). Follow this road as it swings right at the end of the Market Place and continue to the busy major intersection, which you need to cross. Look for The Royal Oak pub, which is on the right hand side of Eastgate. The bus stop is just about outside the pub. Walk is about 10 minutes.

GETTING to PICKERING by BUS

Bus 840 d. Whitby bus stn for Pickering Eastgate Mo-Sa every 2 hr; Su 4/day last week May-1 Oct; 2/day Apr, May & Oct (57 min)

PICKERING to HELMSLEY

Bus 128 d. Pickering Eastgate for Helmsley Mo-Su about 1/hr (38 min)

PICKERING to EDEN CAMP

If you are travelling from Whitby by Bus 840, you can continue to Eden Camp without changing at Pickering.

Bus 840/842 d. Pickering Eastgate for Eden Camp Mo-Sa 1/hr. Su last week May-1 Oct every 1-2 hr; early May & Oct 3/day. Bus stop is at lane leading to Eden Camp (16 minutes) about 5 minutes' walk from entrance.

Eden Camp

Open daily 10.00-17.00
Cost: A £4.50/Co £3.50/Ch £3.50
Tel. 01653 697 777
W: www.edencamp.co.uk

Telephone ahead to verify you can leave your bags at the reception office.

This museum of World War II is spread over 30 themed huts in an old prisoner of war camp. Walk through a bombed street in London, experience a sinking submarine or a rear gunner's seat in a bomber. Allow at least two hours for your visit.

On a cold windy day this is a very chilly outing! There is a bar and canteen. Appropriately enough, the food may not be great, but it is at least warm!

Return to Pickering Eastgate via Bus 840/842 then take Bus 128 for Helmsley

Day 7 – Helmsley

The town of Helmsley existed before the Norman Conquest and managed to survive William the Conqueror's devastation of the north. The lordship of Helmsley was granted to Walter Espec, one of William's knights, in 1120. Espec developed the castle and granted land for the building of Rievaulx Abbey.

When Espec died in 1154 the land passed to his brother-in-law, Peter de Roos, and remained in that family for over 350 years.

In 1508 the last male de Roos died and the estate went to Sir George Manners. The Manners were on amicable terms with Henry VIII and got a good deal buying Rievaulx Abbey at its dissolution. Improvements to the castle incorporated material from the abbey.

In 1644 Cromwell granted the estate to his commander-in-chief, Thomas Fairfax. The Duke of Buckingham acquired the estate by marrying Fairfax's sister, but he died with debts instead of heirs, so the estate was sold to a London goldsmith, Charles Duncombe, in 1689.

Charles began building the country house that is now Duncombe Park. When he died in 1711, the estate passed to his brother-in-law, Thomas Browne (who changed his name to Duncombe).

Thomas Duncombe II was responsible for the broad grass terrace that is flanked by two temple follies and overlooks Rievaulx Abbey.

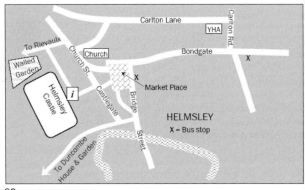

In 1826 the incumbent Duncombe was created Lord Feversham. The house, the walled garden and 450 acres of parkland are owned and maintained by the present Lord Feversham and his family, who still live there.

Helmsley castle and Rievaulx Abbey are now in the care of English Heritage. In 1972 the National Trust bought 60 acres of the estate, including the second Thomas Duncombe's Terrace and Temples.

Take time to explore all the little alleys that lead away from Helmsley market place or you might miss the most photographed bit of the town!

Helmsley Castle, Duncombe Park and the walled garden are all open to the public and within five to ten minutes' walk of the market place.

Rievaulx Abbey and the Terrace are further away, but there is a pleasant walk on mostly level ground, with some steep bits, that takes in both of them. The complete round trip takes at least three hours plus time to visit the two sites. The National Trust welcomes you to picnic on the grassy Terrace.

If you are not up to the walk, plan to visit on Tuesday, Thursday or Saturday when there is a bus service throughout the day.

Helmsley Castle (EH)
Open Apr-Sep daily 10.00-18.00
Oct Th-Mo 10.00-16.00
Cost: A £4.00/Co £3.00/Ch £2.00
Tel. 01439 770 442

The castle overlooks the town from the west. As the town expanded the east tower was heightened to maintain its dominant position.

From the original motte and bailey the castle expanded and changed to meet the needs of the times. Towards the end of the sixteenth century the communal hall, or chamber block, was developed into a private mansion. When, in 1644, Cromwell's forces destroyed most of the castle's defences, the mansion remained intact.

Duncombe Park
Open May-Oct
House by guided tour only at
12.30, 13.30, 14.30 & 15.30
Gardens, parkland, tearoom &
shop 11.00-17.30
Cost: House A £6.50/Co £5.00/
Ch £3.00; Park A £2.00/Ch £1.00
Gardens A £3.50/Co £3.00/
Ch £1.75. EH members House &
Gardens £2.50.
Tel. 01439 770 213
W: www.duncombepark.com

The first Duncombe house was destroyed by fire in 1879, but was rebuilt in its original style.

83

The second Lord Feversham died in World War I, leaving a son too young to take on the responsibilities of a large estate; the house was let as a girls' boarding school and remained so for 60 years.

The present Lord Feversham returned to the house with his wife in 1986 and began a major programme of renovation.

The grounds include a secret garden and an important area of woodland that contains some of the oldest and tallest trees in England. While most of the mature trees are over 250 years old, over 2,000 oak, beech, lime and field maple have been planted in the last decade.

Helmsley Walled Garden
Open daily 10.30-17.00
Cost: A £3.50/Co £2.50/Ch Free
Tel. 01439 771 427
www.helmsleywalledgarden.co.uk

This five-acre walled kitchen garden initiated by Thomas II in 1758 has been undergoing extensive restoration since 1994.

As well as vegetables and herbs, there are 50 varieties of Heritage Yorkshire apples, Victorian vines and the British Clematis Society's National Display Garden. The produce is on sale at the garden.

The Helmsley Attractions Saver gives you entry into Helmsley's top three attractions: Helmsley Castle, Helmsley Walled Garden and Duncombe Park (House and Gardens). The tickets are valid from the date of purchase until October.

THE WALK to RIEVAULX ABBEY
The entire walk is about 5½ miles. Plan to take at least four hours to complete the round trip, including visiting the Abbey and Terrace.

Norman lords and
Anglo-Saxon peasant
©Regia Anglorum

The path is well worn and clearly signposted. Hiking boots or stout walking shoes are advisable as the paths are a bit rough in places, although generally level.

Follow the lane called Cleveland Way and signposted "Cleveland Way & Footpath to Rievaulx" (see street plan). The lane becomes a stone track that runs along the left hand edge of a couple of fields. Where the path turns left look back for a good view of Helmsley Castle.

After you have been through some woods the path turns grassy for a short distance, but is still clear. When you see a yellow sandstone building on the right cross the gravel lane that intersects your path and continue straight ahead. Within more woods there will be another well-worn track crossing yours, but keep going straight ahead. This is the only part not signposted.

When you reach a road turn left and follow the path on the left side, signposted "Rievaulx 1 mile". The path peters out after a while, so just keep following the road. When you see a hump back bridge ahead, look right for a view of the Abbey. Just before the bridge, follow the road to the right to the Abbey parking lot.

CONTINUE to
TERRACE & TEMPLES
Continue along the same road past the abbey, around a couple of curves and through a small hamlet with a small church on the right. Shortly after the road goes uphill out of the hamlet start looking on your right for a narrow path through the ground cover and a sign that says "Footpath to Terrace and Temples 10.30–17.00". The path is narrow, steep, with hairpin bends and seems to go on forever, but eventually puts you just to the right of the entrance to the terrace.

RETURN TO HELMSLEY
Either retrace your steps, or continuing along the drive to the

Helmsley in April

B1257. Turn right and walk the two miles downhill to Helmsley. Although the road is busy, there is a wide grass verge on one side or the other all the way into town. Just watch your footing as the ground is a bit uneven.

BY BUS to RIEVAULX ABBEY
Bus 198 d. Helmsley Market Place for Rievaulx Abbey Tu, Th, Sa 4/day (10 min)

Rievaulx Abbey (EH)

Open Apr-Sep daily 10.00-18.00
Oct Th-Mo 10.00-16.00
Cost: A £4.00/Co £3.00/Ch £2.00
Tel. 01439 798 228

In 1113, when the Cistercian order was still young and idealistic, an aristocrat by the name of Bernard entered Cistercium as a novice. Three years later he was abbot of a daughter house at Clairvaux. Under Bernard's leadership, Clairvaux seeded more houses and in 1131 Bernard eyed northern England and Scotland for the next stage of Cistercian expansionism.

In March 1132, twelve monks and their abbot, William, left Clairvaux for Yorkshire. They started building at Rievaulx on a narrow stretch of flat ground between the river Rye and a steep hillside. The layout of the land was a problem: churches are usually built along an east-west axis with the altar at the east, but the church at Rievaulx had to be rotated almost ninety degrees to fit the available space. Rievaulx has its own liturgical north.

In 1143, a rival order of monks settled on the opposite bank of the Rye. The two abbeys celebrated their offices at different times so the longed-for serenity was shattered at inappropriate moments by the ringing of bells. The Cistercians prevailed and soon had the valley to themselves. In the process they redirected the Rye to provide more room for the abbey buildings, although it was too late to realign the church.

Rievaulx followed the now-familiar pattern: over-expansion, debt, sheep scab, plundering Scots and the Black Death followed by revitalisation.

Rievaulx Abbey surrendered to Henry VIII on 3 December 1538 and shared much the same fate as Fountains: it became a romantic ruin enhancing the view from the terrace above.

An early abbot described Rievaulx as, "everywhere peace, everywhere serenity and a marvellous freedom from the tumult of the world" – but only if you arrive before the crowds!

Terrace and Temples (NT)
Open daily Apr-Sep 10.30-18.00
Oct 10.30-17.00. Ionic temple
closed 13.00-14.00
Cost: A £3.80/Ch £2.00
Tel. 01439 798 340
E: nunningtonhall
@nationaltrust.org.uk

The half-mile long terrace and its two temples were part of the landscaped park of Duncombe. The long stretch of flat grass overlooks the Rye valley and Rievaulx Abbey. At the north end is an Ionic Temple used as a banqueting hall; at the south end is a Tuscan Temple.

Getting Home

Bus 31X d. Helmsley for York Mo-Sa 2/day (1¼hr). Bus 31 d. Helmsley in evening for Easingwold to connect with York bus (1½ hr). Buses terminate at York Exhibition Square. A very scenic route over moors and into small villages. A few minutes after leaving Helmsley, look out on the left for a good view of Byland Abbey.

Su Bus 128 d. Helmsley for Pickering 1/hr

Bus 840, 842 d. Pickering for Malton and connection to Bus 843, 845 to York 4/day last week May to 1 Oct, 3/day Apr, May & Oct.

Highlights of Tour 3

- Mainline Rail Station: Carlisle
    - Day 1 – Travel to Appleby or Kirkby Stephen via Eden Ostrich World at Langwathby
  - Overnight Appleby-in-Westmorland or Kirkby Stephen
    - Day 2/3 – Malham Cove, Gordale Scar, Malham Tarn
- Overnight Malham
    - Day 3 – Travel to Haworth via Skipton for Castle
- Three nights in Haworth
    - Days 4 & 5 – Brontë Parsonage. Day trips to Hebden Bridge for Hardcastle Crags and to Saltaire Village
- Two nights in Marsden or Slaithwaite
    - Days 6 & 7 – Marsden Moor Estate, Standedge Canal Tunnel. Day trips to National Coal Mining Museum and/or Yorkshire Sculpture Park
- Mainline Railway Station: Huddersfield

Tour 3 – The Eden Valley & West Yorkshire

The tour begins in Carlisle, the northern terminus of the most spectacular journey by rail in England: along the Settle-Carlisle line.

From Carlisle the line follows the River Eden between the mountains of Cumbria and the North Pennines, then ploughs over and through the Yorkshire Dales before dropping into Ribblesdale at Settle. The tour continues along the Ribble and Aire valleys,

Tunnel End, Marsden

climbs again into the South Pennines, then heads through the green bottleneck separating Manchester from Huddersfield into the northern tip of the Peak District.

This narrow strip of England does not exactly rank high in most tourists' wish lists. The Lake District overshadows the Eden Valley, while Huddersfied, Bradford and Leeds hardly contribute to west Yorkshire's appeal. Yet there is scenic beauty and drama galore if you know where to look.

The itinerary includes a night in the Eden Valley market town of horse fair fame: Appleby-in-Westmorland. There is a stay in the village of Marsden with a hike to Gordale Scar, Malham Cove (an area of rare limestone pavement) and the Malham Tarn reserve and bird sanctuary. The Scar and tarn are also accessible by bus.

There is time to explore Skipton Castle before picking up the Keighley and Worth Valley Steam Railway to Haworth, home of the Brontë family. From here you can wander the moors seeking inspiration for your own literary legacy or explore some romantically ruined industrial heritage at Hardcastle Crags, now a place of streams, ravines and hairy wood ants, close to the mill town of Hebden Bridge.

On to Marsden for more hikes, dramatic landforms, bird watching and some extraordinary Victorian engineering. You can pursue the industrial motif with a visit to a coal mining museum or increase your culture count at the Yorkshire Sculpture Park.

No stately homes and gardens on this trip: just a medieval castle, fascinating industrial heritage in scenic settings and some splendid walks and hikes.

Accommodation (see page 10 for abbreviations)

APPLEBY-IN-WESTMORLAND, Cumbria – 1 night
Bongate House, Appleby-in-Westmorland CA16 6UE
Tel. 017683 51245
E: information@bongatehouse.co.uk   W: www.bongatehouse.co.uk
Rooms (£pppn): 1Ss, 2Ts/Ds (£21.50); 5Te/De (£25)

Old Hall Farmhouse, Bongate, Appleby-in-Westmorland CA16 6HW
Tel. 0800 035 0422; E: bandbinfo@oldhallfarmhouse.co.uk
W: www.oldhallfarmhouse.co.uk
Rooms (£pppn): 2Te/De, 1De (£25); S in Te/De £35-£45

YHA, Market St, Kirkby Stephen CA17 4QQ
Tel 0870 770 5904; Int (+44) 17683 71793
E: kirkbystephen@yha.org.uk
Cost: £11.00/£8.00
Open Apr-Jun, Sep-Oct: Tu-Sa, BH Su; Jul, Aug daily
Rec. 8.00-10.00, 17.00-22.00; Washer & drying room
One of the better YHA dinners!

MALHAM, North Yorkshire – 1 or 2 nights
YHA, Malham, Skipton, N. Yorks. BD23 4DE
Tel. 0870 770 5946; Int (+44) 1729 830 321
E: malham@yha.org.uk
Cost: £12.50/£9.00
Open daily; Rec. 8.00-10:00; 17.00-22.00; Laundry

Miresfield Farm B&B, Malham, Skipton BD23 4DA
Tel. 01729 830 414
E: info@miresfield-farm.com   W: www.miresfield-farm.com
Rooms (£pppn 2006) 10Te/De (£30); S in Te/De £35-£40

Eastwood House B&B, Malham, Skipton BD23 4DA
Tel. 01729 830 409; E: eastwood-house@hotmail.com
Rooms (£pppn): 2Fe (used as S £35; D £25; F £20)

HAWORTH, West Yorkshire – 3 nights
YHA, Longlands Drive, Lees Lane, Haworth BD22 8RT
Tel. UK 0870 770 5858; Int (+44) 1535 642 234
E: haworth@yha.org.uk
Cost: £12.50/£9.00
Open daily; Rec. 7.30-22.30; Laundry

The Fleece Inn, 67 Main Street, Haworth BD22 8DA
Tel. 01535 642 172; W. www.timothytaylor.co.uk/fleeceinn
Rooms (£/room): 2Se (£35); 4De (£60); 1Te (£60)

Rookery Nook Cottages, 6 Church St., Haworth BD22 8DR
Tel. 01535 640 873
Rooms (£/room): S (£12.50-£22.50); D/T (£25-£45); F £45

MARSDEN/ SLAITHWAITE, West Yorkshire – 2 nights
Throstle Nest Cottage B&B, 3 Old Mount Road, Marsden
Huddersfield HD7 6DU
Tel. 01484 846 371
E: throstlenest@btopenworld.com   W: throstle-nest.co.uk
Rooms (£pppn): 1 std room with 3 S beds, min. stay 2 night (£28)

Pear Tree Cottage, 18 Grange Avenue, Marsden
Huddersfield HD7 6AQ
Tel. 01484 847 518   E: peartreecottage@jgoodall.fsnet.co.uk
W: www.mysite.wanadoo-members.co.uk/pear_tree_cottage
Rooms (£pppn): 1Spb (£25)

Mrs Diane Hawkins, 4 Ingfield, Manchester Road, Marsden HD7 6ET
Tel. 01484 847 770
Rooms (£pppn): 1Ds (£22.50); S in Ds £25.00
Note: This property is not inspected.

Day 1 – Carlisle to Appleby-in-Westmorland

Mainline rail station: CARLISLE
For more information on Carlisle, see page 141.

The Settle-Carlisle railway is awe-inspiring – both scenically and technically. It has more viaducts and tunnels than any other route in England.

Before the Settle-Carlisle line existed, Midland Railway shared the London & North Western Railway's west coast line, an arrangement so unsatisfactory that in 1869 Midland began building a high speed freight and passenger line under the direction of engineer John Crossley. High speed means no meandering around hills: through and over does the trick.

Six years, 72 miles of track, fourteen tunnels and twenty viaducts later the Settle-Carlisle line opened for freight traffic. Nine months on, the first passenger train headed north.

From Carlisle the train heads south to the Eden Valley and Langwathby, the stop for the Eden Ostrich World.

THE SETTLE-CARLISLE LINE
Trains d. Carlisle Mo-Fr 5/day; Sa 6/day; Su 3-4/day

Eden Ostrich World
Open daily 10.00-17.00
Cost: A £4.50/Co £3.75/Ch £3.50
Tel. 01768 881 771
W: www.ostrich-world.com

GETTING to EDEN OSTRICH WORLD
Alight at Langwathby (27 min). Be careful of the nettles at the platform gate. Walk down the hill, turn left under the railway bridge and shortly turn right following the white-on-brown sign for Eden Ostrich World. Turn left down the lane just before the church and graveyard, then look diagonally across the two village greens to the right, where you will see the entrance. A 10-minute walk.

Out of peak tourist season this working farm at first appears desolate and deserted, but don't be put off. Away from the utilitarian farmyard the views over the rolling green fields are lovely, while strolling by the paddocks of horses, ponies, sheep, deer and ostriches is both entertaining and relaxing. There is a riverside walk in a Site of Special Scientific Interest.

Back in the farmyard, the sheep are milked at 14.00, an exercise in efficient crowd management – of the sheep, not the visitors! There are lots of fun-looking activities for children.

The attraction is pleasant and interesting, but best avoided on a rainy day.

GETTING to APPLEBY-IN-WESTMORLAND
Return to the rail station to continue down the line to Appleby-in-Westmorland (15 min from Langwathby).

From Appleby railway station turn left down Station Road and left again at the T-junction with The

Eden Ostrich World

Sands. Cross the bridge on the right then turn left into Borough-gate. The TIC will be on your right.

Appleby-in-Westmorland

Where the River Eden winds around a tight S-bend sits the old market town of Appleby. Once the county seat of Westmorland, Appleby is best known for its annual Horse Fair, which runs for one week and ends on the second Wednesday in June.

Since receiving its charter from James II in 1685, this huge gypsy gathering has been attracting all sorts of horsemen – an eccentric subset of humanity, to put it mildly – to a boisterous week of trading and dealing in the hope of finding the perfect, or at least a suitable, horse. Accommodation during the fair is booked a year or more in advance. Bear that in mind when planning your holiday!

Less flamboyant, but just as influential on the history of Appleby, is Lady Anne Clifford (1590-1676). A fighter and philanthropist, Lady Anne was responsible for the restoration of many churches and castles in Westmorland, where she was High Sheriff from 1657 to 1658.

She fortified the old Norman castle at Appleby against the forces of Cromwell during the Civil War and built the Hospital of St Anne, a row of almshouses near the entrance to the castle. More about Lady Anne is told at Skipton Castle.

Boroughgate is the primary axis of Appleby. At the north end, near the TIC and the Low Cross, is St. Lawrence Church, which Lady Anne Clifford restored and where she is buried.

The earliest part of the church is the lower section of the tower, which dates from the twelfth century. The remainder of the building was burned by raiding Scots in 1388 and was rebuilt and extended over the succeeding centuries.

Of geological rather than ecclesiastical interest is the 19^{th}C font: embedded in the marble are more fossils than you can count.

The Saturday market is held around the Low Cross.

Boroughgate leads south to the High Cross, St. Anne's Hospital and the Norman Castle. The castle and grounds are privately owned and at the time of writing were closed to the public for health and safety reasons.

Overnight in Appleby-in-Westmorland or continue to Kirkby Stephen for the youth hostel.

GETTING to
KIRKBY STEPHEN YHA

Grand Prix Bus 563 d. Appleby The Sands (look for the bus stop across the road from the bridge) for Kirkby Stephen (The Square – very close to YHA) Mo-Sa every 2-3 hr (28 min) No Su service.

By train is not recommended. From Kirkby Stephen station it is a 1½ mile walk along a busy road with no pavement. If you really want to do this, walk down the long, moderately steep hill, follow the road into the town and keep going until you see the Youth Hostel (inside an old Methodist Chapel) on left. ½ hr walk. You will be able to return to the rail station by bus in the morning.

Day 2 – Appleby-in-Westmorland to Malham

Getting to Malham is time critical: on weekdays there are two daily buses; on weekends, four. If you are staying in Malham just one night, catch the mid-afternoon postbus, which will get you there in time for a good three-hour walk before dinner.

GETTING to MALHAM
Continue south on the Settle-Carlisle line.

[FROM KIRKBY STEPHEN YHA to KIRKBY STEPHEN RAIL STATION Take a bus!
Bus 571 d. Kirkby Stephen (outside HSBC) for rail stn Mo-Sa thrice in a.m. Bus 564 d. Kirkby Stephen (Market Square) for end of Station Approach Mo-Sa twice in a.m. and about noon. No Su service.]

Alight at Gargrave (1 hr) or Skipton (1¼ hr). Not all trains stop at Gargrave, a pretty village with a river and a tea room across from the bus stop. Buses from Skipton to Malham stop at Gargrave.

From Appleby the Settle-Carlisle railway, which we are travelling in reverse, starts the long climb to Ais Gill Summit on the border between Cumbria and Yorkshire. The best of the spectacular views along this stretch are on the east (left) side of the train.

After the train emerges from the first tunnel after Kirkby Stephen start looking down to the left for a glimpse of the ruined Pendragon Castle. Restored by Lady Anne Clifford, the castle is supposedly the home of King Arthur's father, Uther Pendragon, but is more likely a 12th C defence against the Scots.

One more viaduct, then Ais Gill, the highest point on the line at 1,169 feet above sea level. Nearby is Hell Gill Beck, the source of the Eden. Ponder the implications of that, if you will.

Two viaducts and a tunnel after Dent, the highest mainline station in England, look out for the 24 arches of the splendid Ribblehead Viaduct. The train continues downhill to Settle and proceeds to Gargrave and Skipton where you alight for the bus to Malham.

From Gargrave rail station turn left and follow the road into the village, past the church on the right, over the bridge and immediately right is the square and bus stop (5 min). The stop is the one close to the river, not outside the tea room across the road.

From Skipton rail station turn right into Broughton Road and stick to it as it changes first to Belmont Street then to Swadford Street. About half a mile from the station turn right into Keighley Road and Skipton bus station is on the right (10 min)

From Skipton bus stn and Gargrave Mo-Fr: The Royal Mail *Postbus d. for Malham mid-p.m.

Bus 210 d. late p.m.
Sa, Su/BH: Bus 210, 843, 804 4/day (25 min from Gargrave, 40 min from Skipton).

*The Post Bus is red. It may not turn into the bus stop at Gargrave but does slow down, so when you see it coming, wave it down.

Malham is a beautiful but not very peaceful little village in the Yorkshire Dales National Park. Close by are Gordale Scar, Malham Cove and Malham Tarn, areas of special geological and ornithological interest, much visited by hikers, naturalists and swarms of school children. It gets very crowded in summer and is not exactly lonely the rest of the year, so book your accommodation well in advance.

In order to visit all three fascinating sites, plan for a full-day outing and spend two nights in Malham. For the less ambitious or more pressed for time a short half day walk that leaves out Malham Tarn is possible to complete after arriving by the mid-afternoon postbus. For that you need stay only one night.

The following walk takes in Gordale Scar, the spectacular waterfall and gorge that was created by glacial rivers over the last million or so years, and the limestone pavement on the cliff top at Malham Cove.

To see the above and Malham Tarn Reserve and Bird Sanctuary buy the *Malham Trail* leaflet from the National Park Centre (£1.00), as this describes the nine-mile walk and points of interest. All sales support the work of the National Parks.

An easier way to get to the tarn on weekends and Bank Holidays is to take the National Trust Shuttle from Malham to the Tarn. The shuttle leaves the National Park Centre in Malham every half-hour.

WALK to JANET'S FOSS, GORDALE SCAR and MALHAM COVE

From the National Park Visitor Centre, turn left toward the village and cross the road to The Smithy. Go behind this small stone building, over the stone footbridge and along the path to the right. There is a sign for Pennine Way, Janet's Foss and Gordale Scar.

Where there are two kissing gates side by side in a wall, take the left path towards the small stone barn and through another kissing gate. You will soon see Gordale Beck, a small stream, on your right.

Follow the path into the National Trust Malham Woods, pass a couple of "money trees" (a money tree is an old tree stump with hundreds of coins jammed into its

bark) and arrive at Janet's Foss. "Foss" is Norse for waterfall and Janet is queen of the fairies who live behind the fall.

Follow the path up to the left of the Foss, turn right on the road and continue over the stone bridge. Look out on your left for a wide gate and sign for Gordale Scar. Follow the wide gravel path about ¼ mile.

Don't be put off by signs warning of a steep, difficult climb. No climbing is required. As you get closer, look out for springs bubbling out of the grass.

When you have gone as far into the gorge as you like, return to the stone bridge back on the road and look for the sign pointing to Malham Cove on your right.

From here to Malham Cove the path varies from gravel or stone to faintly worn grass. At least the signs all point in the right direc-

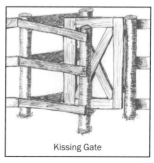

Kissing Gate

97

tion! Head gradually uphill across a couple of large fields to another road. Turn right and use the ladder stile to go over the wall on the far side of the road. Follow the signs for Malham Cove, bearing left.

The 'cove' is a horseshoe-shaped cliff about 230' high. You will be on top of the cliff standing on a bizarre limestone pavement of large blocks and deep crevices (clints and grykes respectively) formed since the last ice age 12,000 years ago. The crevices create ideal growing conditions for some rare plant species.

Aim for the long curving flight of stone steps on the far side of the horseshoe. Descend the steps, turn right on the gravel path and continue to the road. Turn left and you will return to the village.

For most of the walk the path is wide, gravelled and hard to miss, but there are some rough bits and some slippery bits. Please read the walking precautions on page 183.

This walk is about 4¼ miles. Allow about 2 ½ to 3 hours.

Overnight in Malham.

Day 3 – Malham – Skipton – Haworth

The trip from Malham to Haworth (pr. How-urth), home of the Brontë sisters, requires a change of bus at Skipton. This is a good chance to visit Lady Anne Clifford's Skipton Castle. There is a tea room in the grounds.

From Skipton there are frequent train and bus services to Keighley (pr. Keithley), the terminus of the Keighley & Worth Valley Railway (KWVR), which runs diesel and steam trains to Haworth on weekends and school holidays. A bus service also runs from Keighley to Haworth.

GETTING to SKIPTON
Mo-Fr: Bus 210 d. Malham for

Skipton early a.m. and late p.m. The Postbus d. Malham in the morning but is a little erratic. Your B&B host or Youth Hostel will advise you on how to catch it. It passes through Malham a second time about ¾ hr after the first. If you catch it the first time you get a fascinating drive to outlying farms, but be warned: this is definitely a *Motion Sickness Alert!*

Sa, Su/BH: Bus 210, 843, 804 d. Malham for Skipton 4/day (35 min) To continue to Haworth without visiting the castle, alight at the bus station.

For Skipton Castle alight in the town centre and walk up High

Street following the remarkably accurate signs for the castle (5 min)

Skipton Castle

Open Mo-Sa 10.00, Su 12.00. Last admission 18.00 (16.00 Oct)
Cost: A £5.20/Co £4.60/Ch £2.70
Tel. 01756 792442
W: www.skiptoncastle.co.uk

The first recorded castle on the site was built of timber shortly after 1090 as part of William the Conqueror's campaign to subdue the north. This no longer exists and the earliest remains are the two Norman towers flanking the projecting 17thC entrance (once a bridge and portcullis) and the interior arch leading to the Conduit Court.

The castle was granted to Robert Clifford in 1310. It remained the principal seat of the Clifford family until the death of Lady Anne Clifford in 1676.

Lady Anne was born in Skipton Castle in 1590. Her father, who died when she was fifteen, had entailed the Clifford estates to his offspring regardless of gender. An entail usually goes through the male line and consists of property that, in effect, belongs to future generations of the family and cannot be sold or given away. Lady Anne's uncle, cousin and the courts ignored the gender stipula-

tion, so she did not come into her inheritance until her cousin died in 1643.

Meanwhile, she married the Earl of Dorset in 1609. He died in 1624 and she married, six years later, the Earl of Pembroke and Montgomery, a Parliamentarian. Lady Anne was a Royalist. The earl died in 1649.

Lady Anne's marriages had not been happy, but her husbands had been rich. With the Clifford estates finally her own, she could enjoy life as a wealthy widow.

During the Civil War (1642-1649) Skipton castle held loyal to the Stuarts and withstood Cromwell's siege for three years. In 1648 the Royalists reoccupied the castle but were again ejected and the castle was "pulld downe and demolisht, allmost to the foundacon, by the command of the parliament…" [inscription over main entrance]

Lady Anne was able to persuade Cromwell to let her rebuild it with the proviso it not be strong enough to withstand another siege. So it is thanks to Lady Anne that Skipton is one of the few medieval castles standing in good repair.

The entry fee includes a cleverly illustrated one-sheet guide that leads you from room to room, continually returning to the lovely

Conduit Courtyard, still dominated by the yew tree that Lady Anne planted in 1659. Illustrated informational boards in most of the rooms supplement the guide.

Take a good look at the ticket office, an early 17thC Shell Room or Grotto. The only other room of this nature is at Woburn Abbey.

Caution: The steps to the dungeon are worn: not obvious as the lighting is quite dim.

Return to Skipton bus station to continue to Haworth.

Haworth

Haworth consists of the old village and the town. The village runs up the side of a steep hill and has the cobbled streets, the church, the Brontë parsonage, the tea rooms and the views. The town on the opposite hill has nothing much at all.

The KWVR station lies in the valley, about a quarter mile from the top of the cobbled Main Street a short walk, but a steep one.

The accommodation listed for Haworth, with the exception of the Youth Hostel, is within the old village. The Youth Hostel is about a mile in the opposite direction.

Three nights in Haworth.

GETTING to HAWORTH by BUS
From Skipton Castle walk down High Street, turn right into Swadford Street (the first major road) and almost immediately left into Keighley Road. The bus station is on the right (10 min)

Bus 66, 67, 68 d. Skipton bus stn for Keighley bus stn Mo-Sa 2/hr; Su/BH Bus 67A 1/hr (32 min)

Bus 663, 664, 665 d. Keighley bus stn for Haworth Mo-Sa 3/hr; Su/BH 2/hr (18 min)

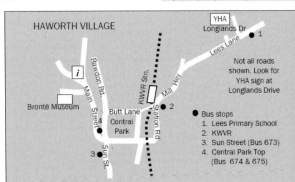

For accommodation in Haworth village: The buses stop at the KWVR station then turn right and head uphill. At the top Bus 663 turns left and Buses 664 and 665 turn right. The stop is immediately after the turn. See map at left. You can see the cobbled Main Street of the Village from the bus stop.

For Haworth YHA ask for the youth hostel or Lees Primary School, cross the road, turn left and look out on the right for Longlands Drive and the YHA sign.

Haworth Village Main Street

GETTING to HAWORTH by TRAIN From Skipton Castle walk down High Street, turn right into Swadford Street and walk about half a mile to the railway station on the left.

Trains d. Skipton for Keighley Mo-Sa 4-5/hr; Su 1-2/hr (10-13 min)

KWVR d. Keighley rail station platform 4 Sa, Su, BH and school holidays. Times vary with season (15 min) Timetables are available at any TIC in the area or visit www.kwvr.co.uk or Tel. 01535 645214.

The KWVR is more an outing than a simple journey. There is a Museum of Railway Travel at Ingrow West (open daily 11.00-14.30) admission included with Day Rover ticket or A£1.50/CoCh £1.00.
The train stops at Damens, Britain's smallest rail station and at Oakworth, the location for the film *The Railway Children*.

From the KWVR station cross the footbridge over the tracks, turn right up the steep cobbled Butt Lane, cross the paved road, through a cobbled car park and a gap in the wall, then turn right again into Main Street (another steep hill).

Day 4 – Haworth & Hebden Bridge

Haworth is quite small and can be explored in half a day or so, depending on your preferences. It is also a pleasant and convenient base for trips to the National Trust woodland estate of Hardcastle Crags and to the Victorian "model village" of Saltaire.

Note: Write or e-mail the National Trust for the Hardcastle Crags Events & Waymarked Trails leaflet. They are available at the property, but the entrance is unattended and there may be none. Contact information is on page 104.

The Brontë Family

The story of the Brontë family is nearly as dark as the novels of Charlotte, Emily and Anne.

Their father, Patrick Brontë, married Maria Branwell in 1812.

In the following eight years Maria produced six children. The last, Anne, was born in January 1820, three months before the family moved to the parsonage in Haworth. Eighteen months later Maria died and her sister moved in to look after the family.

It is hard to imagine now, but in the early nineteenth century Haworth was overcrowded and had a poor water supply and open drains. Forty-one per cent of children born in Haworth died before the age of six. The graveyard today reflects this frightening figure.

In 1824 the four oldest girls, Maria, Elizabeth, Charlotte and Emily, aged ten, nine, eight and six, respectively, were sent to the Clergy Daughters' School in

Graveyard, Haworth Parish Church

Kirkby Lonsdale. Maria and Elizabeth became ill at the school and died within six weeks of each other. Shades of *Jane Eyre*.

For the next quarter century the remaining siblings lived and worked much as others of their class and time: Charlotte, Emily and Anne as governesses or teachers; their brother Branwell as an unsuccessful painter, then as a tutor.

In September 1848 Branwell died, soon followed by Emily in December and Anne in May 1849, all most likely of tuberculosis. Charlotte survived to marry her father's curate in 1854, but she died less than a year later.

Patrick Brontë continued as parson of Haworth church until his death in 1861.

The Brontë memorial is on a wall inside the church where all but Anne are interned in a vault under the floor. Anne was buried in Scarborough,

John Wade, Patrick Brontë's successor, found the church ugly, inconvenient and, what a surprise, unhealthy. Against opposition from Brontë fans, he had it pulled down in 1879 and rebuilt to a simpler plan as seen today. Wade also added the right hand wing of the house in 1878.

Brontë Parsonage Museum

Open daily Apr-Sep 10.00-17.30
Oct 11.00-17.00
Cost: A£4.90/Co £3.60/Ch £1.60
Tel. 01535 642323
W: www.bronte.info

The parsonage was built in 1778 and became the home of the Brontës in 1820.

Much of their furniture and some of their belongings remain in situ with period pieces and reproductions filling the gaps to give a realistic impression of the parsonage as it was during the Brontës' residence.

Until 31 March 2007 the museum also hosts an exhibition of illustrations of the Brontë novels.

The path past the museum continues towards the moors where the Bronte sisters walked drawing inspiration for such novels as *Wuthering Heights.*

Hebden Bridge (half or full day)

The bus route from Haworth to Hebden Bridge goes through the Dales and provides some lovely views.

In spite of having been cleaned and sanitised, the mill town of Hebden Bridge still harbours alleys where washing hangs from wall to wall. It can be a relief, sometimes, to see signs of normal life in supposedly revitalised industrial areas!

The lost industry of Hebden Bridge was textile manufacture. The redundant mill stands by St. George's Square in the centre of the town. This 700 year old building began life as a manorial corn mill. Four hundred years later it was converted to textile mill and now houses shops and cafés.

The town is attractive enough, but the main reason for visiting is to explore Hardcastle Crags.

The property is about 1½ miles from the town centre. There is a pleasant walk, mostly beside Hebden Water (a river, not a lake), and a bus service.

GETTING to HEBDEN BRIDGE
Bus 500 d. Haworth opposite the KWVR station and Sun Street for Hebden Bridge Mo-Su every 2-3 hr with an extra bus on Sa (26 min). Ask to be let off at Albert Street.

To find the TIC: go back up Albert Street, turn right into New Road and the TIC will soon be on your left.

Hardcastle Crags (NT)

Open daily unlimited access
Cost: free
Tel. 01422 844 518
E: hardcastlecrags
@nationaltrust.org.uk
Telephone or E-mail to request a copy of *Hardcastle Crags Events & Waymarked Trails*. Leaflets are also available in the entrance car park.

GETTING to HARDCASTLE CRAGS
Bus H leaves Hebden Bridge New Road (near the TIC) for Hardcastle Crags car park Mo-Su 1/hr
OR
WALK from HEBDEN BRIDGE to HARDCASTLE CRAGS
From Albert Street continue down to St. George's Square. Keep to the left of the square, cross the bridge and turn immediately right into Valley Road. Follow Valley Road as it re-crosses the river and turns sharp left to become Victoria Road. Take the second turn right, then the first turn left into Spring Grove (signposted "Windsor Place leading to Spring Grove"). At the end of Spring Grove cross the footbridge and turn immediately right to follow the riverside path.

Look to your left to see hedge-laying in work. This is how hedgerows begin, with the planting and training of the hedge to form an animal-proof barrier. It provides shade for the sheep or cattle and shelter for a variety of wildlife. It also takes a long time to grow and for many years hedgerows were torn out as they were considered uneconomical. However, their value has been recognised, and they are being replanted in some areas.

When you reach the point where you can either continue straight on or turn right over a footbridge, take the footbridge. Continue with the river on your left, then go up the long flight of stone steps on your right. At the top, turn left and continue until the path intersects the road.

Cross the road and continue up another flight of narrow steps into Hardcastle Crags Spring Wood. Follow the path to the left, then down steps back to the road. Turn right and continue along the road until a lane diverges on the left, signposted "Leading to Lower Mill".

Follow the lane and turn left through a small gate and skirt the sheep field back down to the river. Turn left through another small gate, over the bridge and follow the path to the right. You will eventually arrive at a small car park.

Continue through the car park to the road, turn right, over the bridge and turn left at the junction. The Hardcastle Crags car park is on the right.

Hardcastle Crags has four way-marked paths that wind for about 7½ miles through woods dotted with clues to the area's industrial past: a narrow gauge railway, workers' cottages, a pavilion for skaters, charcoal hearths, an 18thC cotton mill and more. Take a picnic lunch, but look out for the Northern Hairy Wood Ants, another feature of the property. Before heading out, check the Bus H timetable on the post near the car park. You may not be up to the 1½ mile walk back to Hebden Bridge!

Return to Haworth for the night.

Bus 500 d. Hebden Bridge Hope Street for Haworth Mo-Su every 2-3 hr with an extra bus on Sa. (From St. George's Square head back to Albert St. but take the road to the right of Albert St. The stop is directly outside the library)

Saltaire Village

Day 5 – Day trip to Saltaire

Saltaire village was built by mill owner Titus Salt to house the workforce of his new mill. It is a World Heritage Site, demonstrating the type of model village that first started to appear in the late eighteenth century.

Titus Salt was born into the textile industry in 1803 and thrived on it. He started his own mill in 1836 and created new luxury cloths of alpaca wool combined with silk or cotton.

By 1850 Salt owned five mills and was Mayor of Bradford. He used his position and wealth to alleviate the squalid living conditions of his workers by building schools, hospitals and orphanages.

With new equipment and a desire to consolidate his mills, Salt searched for a site that was larger and better supplied with water than was available in Bradford. At the same time he was inspired to build a Utopian town for his workers. A site four miles from Bradford on the Leeds-Liverpool canal beside the Midland Railway and the River Aire met all his requirements; it had space, transportation and power.

The huge new mill opened in 1853. The village of Saltaire was completed fifteen years later with houses for workers, foremen and managers; boarding houses for bachelors, schools, almshouses for the worthy poor, bath houses, a park, church and hospital.

When Salt died in 1876 the business went to his two sons. The mill and the village were never quite the same. Production ceased in 1986 after 133 years of business.

The village, now occupied by 21^{st}C workers, has been preserved within the town of Saltaire: a successful example of a working heritage.

The disused mill has been rejuvenated and the park continues to provide a place for recreation and relaxation.

GETTING to SALTAIRE
KWVR from Haworth to Keighley (20 min)
OR
Bus 663, 664, 665 d. Haworth opposite KWVR for Keighley Mo-Sa 3/hr; Su/BH 2/hr (18 min)

MetroTrain d. Keighley rail stn for Saltaire Mo-Sa 4+/hr; Su 1-2/hr (9 min)

From Saltaire station, turn right into Victoria Road, over the railway bridge, cross the narrow cobbled Albert Terrace and look for the '*i*' sign one or two shops up on the right. From there you can buy *Saltaire Trail* (£1.50), an excellent booklet providing a guided walk of the area with the history and points of interest. The main part of the walk, which returns you to the railway bridge, takes about an hour.

GOOD EATING

At the corner of Lower School Road and Victoria Road, just after the Vigilant Lion statue, is *Massarella Fine Art & Tea Rooms*. Here you can enjoy morning coffee, lunch or afternoon tea and browse through the artwork while you wait.

1853 Gallery & Salts Mill
Open daily 10.00-18.00
Cost: free
Tel. 01274 531 163
W: www.saltsmill.org.uk

Salts Mill is the gargantuan building across Victoria Road from the rail station. It houses Europe's largest collection of work by Bradford-born artist David Hockney: more than 300 pieces on permanent display, plus changing exhibitions and operatic stage sets. There are shops, cafés and restaurants.

Saltaire United Reformed Church
Open Apr-Sep daily 14.00-16.00
Oct Su 14.00-16.00
BH 10.30-16.00
Cost: free

Tel. 01274 597 894
W: www.saltaireurc.info

Opposite Salts Mill and hard to miss, the church is like an ornamental salt shaker sitting on top of an otherwise classical rotunda. The interior is as extravagant as the village is not: a Victorian tabernacle of middle class wealth and piety in coloured marble.

Roberts Park
At the bottom of Victoria Road, just over the Leeds & Liverpool Canal, is Robert's Park, intended by Salt for the "moral and social elevation of the working class". Horses, asses, mules, unaccompanied children and unleashed dogs were denied admittance. Working class or not, today you can enjoy the park without concern for your moral or social elevation!

Shipley Glen Cable Tramway
Open Apr-Sep Sa 13.00-17.00; Su 12.00-18.00; Oct Sa,Su 12.00-17.00
Cost (return): A 80p/CoCh 50p
Tel. 01274 589010
W: www.glentramway.co.uk

A sign-posted path within Roberts Park leads to this Victorian cable tramway. Built in 1895, the original cars still trundle up and down the quarter-mile hill to the hundred-year old pleasure grounds, woods and open moorland at the top.

Pleasure Grounds & Children's Fun Fair

Open School holidays and Sa 12.00-17.00; Su 11.00-18.00 BH 10.00-18.00
Admission free, charge for rides.
Tel. 01274 580 622

Alternatively, follow the canal for three miles to the 18thC Three and Five Rise Locks at Bingley. You can pick up the train to Keighley from Bingley.

Day 6 – Marsden (or Slaithwaite)

From the Pennines and Airedale we head into the Peak District.

Seven miles west of Huddersfield is the town of Marsden. Once fouled by the clamour, filth and stench of heavy industry, Marsden's heritage has been sanitized to the point where the smoke stacks

Slaithwaite Mill

and blank-faced factories are really quite attractive in their own kind of way. Indeed, the little town is a lovely place to stay for a day or two.

Before tourism, sheep were all that flourished on the bleak and boggy east slopes of the Peaks. Sheep mean wool and the area developed into a busy centre for the cottage textile industry.

Marsden thrived during the Industrial Revolution. It had the raw material (sheep and water), the skilled labour force (all those spinning and weaving families the new mills would soon put out of business) and the reputation for high quality wool products to support the introduction of large mechanised mills. Transportation to the markets was provided by the Huddersfield Narrow Canal and the developing road network, which were soon to be augmented by the railways.

Heavy mill equipment, iron-hulled canal boats and railways all require iron. Two blacksmiths,

Enoch and James Taylor, saw an opportunity for expansion and created the Marsden Iron Foundry.

When the Luddites, a group who disapproved of mechanisation and the social changes it wrought, set out to destroy the machinery in the mills both their hammers and the machinery they smashed had been manufactured by the Taylor brothers.

As an added bonus, the local sandstone, called Millstone Grit, proved excellent for grinding.

The industry has gone and today Marsden makes an attractive and convenient base for hiking over the 5,000 acres of the Marsden Moor Estate, a property owned by the National Trust.

The town is just half a mile from Tunnel End, the entrance to the longest, highest and deepest canal tunnel in the United Kingdom. *Last of the Summer Wine* and *Where the Heart Is* were filmed at Marsden.

Where the Heart Is was also filmed at Slaithwaite (pr. Slowait), three miles along the canal towards Huddersfield. Slaithwaite experienced the same industrial past as Marsden but is a bit larger and busier. If all the accommodation in Marsden is full Slaithwaite is an entirely acceptable alternative.

In addition to walking or taking a canal trip into the tunnel, the two towns are convenient for trips to the National Coal Mining Museum and the Yorkshire Sculpture Park.

The Huddersfield Narrow Canal, which was re-opened in 2001, flows through the middle of Slaithwaite, past Marsden and into Standedge Tunnel. It makes for a pleasant canal-side walk of not quite an hour between the two towns. Canal buffs should look out for the guillotine gate just west of Slaithwaite. It is the only working

Seven-foot wide narrow boat on the Huddersfield Narrow Canal

109

example on a narrow canal in England.

Two nights in Marsden or Slaithwaite.

GETTING to MARSDEN
Slaithwaite is one stop (6 min) before Marsden on the train from Huddersfield. All bus and train routes serve both. Although there are a lot of changes between Haworth and Marsden, the trains are all quite frequent (except on Sunday) so the journey is not as bad as it may seem below.

KWVR from Haworth to Keighley
OR
Bus 663, 664, 665 d. Haworth opposite KWVR for Keighley Mo-Sa 3/hr, Su/BH 2/hr (18 min)

Train d. Keighley for Leeds Mo-Sa 2-3/hr; Su 1-2/hr (27 min)

Train d. Leeds for Huddersfield Mo-Sa 4+/hr; Su 1-2/hr (18 -40 min depending on the service)
Note: On Su the slow trains go direct to Slaithwaite and Marsden from Leeds

Train d. Huddersfield for Marsden Mo-Sa 1/hr; Su every 2 hr (13 min)

Marsden Moor Estate (NT)

Open Estate unlimited access
Exhibition daily 9.00-17.00
Estate Office, The Old Goods Yard, Station Road, Marsden
W. Yorks. HD7 6DH
Tel. 01484 847016

E: marsdenmoor
@nationaltrust.org.uk

Marsden Moor Estate is a Site of Special Scientific Interest incorporating the northern part of the Peak District National Park. These 5,685 acres of heather and moss, reservoirs, valleys and crags provide a home for such birds as the kestrel, curlew, red grouse, dunlin and skylark. There is a bronze age burial site, Millstone Grit quarries, a Roman road, canal tunnel and more.

The National Trust has prepared a *Guide to the Marsden Moor Estate* describing six walks that range from just under three miles to eight miles. Please read the Tips for Safe Hiking on page 183.

The National Trust has also prepared a *Guide to Marsden and Tunnel End*. Both are available **free** from the Estate Office adjacent to Marsden railway station, either in person or by sending a self-addressed envelope.

Canal-side Walks

Even for the least energetic, the half-mile stroll to Tunnel End is easy and very rewarding.

A Water-Taxi service between Marsden Railway Station and the Standedge (pr. "Stannidge") Tunnel at Tunnel End is operated weekends and bank holidays by the Huddersfield Canal Society, subject to volunteer availability.

To work up a bit of an appetite, follow the broad, level path beside the canal to Slaithwaite (three miles) for an elegant little lunch on a traditional canal boat.

GOOD EATING IN SLAITHWAITE

The *Moonraker Floating Tea Rooms* are in a converted narrow boat on the canal in Slaithwaite. They offer reasonably priced and tasty light lunches and snacks.

Standedge Visitor Centre

Open Visitor Centre:
Apr-Sep Sa, Su/BH; mid-Jul-Aug daily: 10.00-16.30
Boat trips: Apr-Sep Sa, Su/BH at 11.00, 11.45, 12.30, 13.45, 14.30, 15.15.
Cost: Interpretation Centre free
Boat trips: A £2.00/Co £1.50/Ch £1.00
Tel. 01484 844 298
W: www.standedge.co.uk

The visitor centre at Tunnel End features a small but interesting exhibition on canals, the Huddersfield Canal and the Standedge Tunnel in particular. Boat trips 500 metres into the tunnel are available.

Standedge Tunnel cuts through nearly 3½ miles of the Pennines from Marsden to Diggle and is the longest, deepest and highest canal tunnel in England. It is 645 feet above sea level and is 648 feet below the surface.

The tunnel was completed in 1811 under the aegis of Thomas Telford. It took sixteen years to build. The canal was restored and reopened on 1 May 2001 by Lily Turner, the daughter of David Whitehead, the fastest legger through the tunnel (in 1914). Because canal tunnels were too narrow to include a tow path, the horses were led over the top while a legger or two "walked" the boats through, as shown below.

Narrow boats still traverse the tunnel but not by legging it!

Legger in Standedge Tunnel

111

A Bit About Canals

Canals flourished because of the Industrial Revolution. The vastly increased traffic of raw material and manufactured goods between mines, factories and ports proved too much for the existing network of muddy roads and silted-up rivers. In 1761 the Duke of Bridgewater built a canal linking his coal mine with the port of Liverpool and the manufacturing city of Manchester, thus starting a canal-building boom.

However, the railways soon began to take business from the canals, which gradually fell into disrepair.

Shortly after World War II, canal boat holidays became popular.

Canal restoration and river clearance began and continue. There are currently 2,000 miles of navigable inland waterways throughout much of England and parts of Wales.

The early narrow boats and barges had been towed by horses, hence all those lovely canal-side paths that provide such peaceful walks.

Narrow boats, not to be confused with barges, which are much wider, are constructed of iron and wood, are 70 feet long and seven feet wide. They are designed specifically for transporting freight along the narrow canals and locks that were designed to keep water loss to a minimum.

Day 7 – Day trips from Marsden/Slaithwaite

Both the **National Coal Mining Museum (NCM)** and the **Yorkshire Sculpture Park** are a train or bus ride from Marsden to Huddersfield then a thirty- to forty-minute bus journey from there. The connections are quite good and the attractions are near the bus stops.

Allow at least a half-day with lunch for each outing. There is a great deal to see and do at the NCM and the Sculpture Park offers interesting walks and exhibitions. Both provide indoor features for wet days and attractive picnic spots for sunny ones.

Although geographically close, there is no bus connecting the two, so on any given day you'll really only be able to visit one.

GETTING to
HUDDERSFIELD BUS STATION
Bus 184, 350, 351, 352 d. Marsden for Huddersfield Mo-Sa 5/hr; Su every 2/hr (31 min)

MetroTrain d. Marsden for Huddersfield Mo-Sa 1/hr; Su every 2 hr (13 min). From Huddersfield rail station turn right immediately

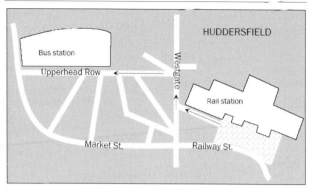

in front of the building then right again into Westgate and left into Upperhead Row (see map). These two roads are *very* busy. The bus station is a five-minute walk from the rail station.

The National Coal Mining Museum for England
Open daily 10.00-17.00
Cost: free
Tel. 01924 848806
W: www.ncm.org.uk

GETTING THERE
Bus 232 d. Huddersfield bus stn for Overton Mo-Su 1/hr (40 min)
Ask for the Coal Mining Museum and you will be dropped off at The Reindeer pub near Overton.

From The Reindeer, walk about 100 yards in the same direction as the bus and turn left down the narrow lane. The museum is across the busy road at the bottom of the hill with the visitor centre uphill to the left. (10 min walk to visitor centre)

This excellent museum makes use of the Caphouse Colliery and Hope Pit, which closed in the 1980s. The visitor centre relates the stories of miners and their families thus creating a vivid picture of what mine work was like before and after the advent of modern machinery.

The stories are enhanced by the realities of the coal screening plant, steam winding house, control room, boiler house, pithead baths, haulage house and stables.

The 1¼ hour underground tour is very popular, so book it at the visitor centre as soon as you arrive. Children must be five years or older and accompanied by an

113

adult. Warm clothes and sturdy shoes are necessary. Battery operated equipment is not allowed. Hardhats and lamps are provided. A local miner will escort you down the 460 foot shaft in a cage and through a labyrinth of tunnels. This is not for the claustrophobic.

There is a little stable yard for the retired pit ponies, who are enjoying their hard-earned rest (possibly in a field when you drop by), a nature trail, rides on a mining train and a playground.

Allow about three to four hours for the visit. There is a picnic area, café serving plain but entirely edible food, and a gift shop.

If your time is limited, you could visit the Coal Mining Museum as a side trip on your homeward journey but there is no official luggage storage and limited space behind the desk. Security precautions are getting ever more stringent so it would be best to telephone ahead to check the policy before visiting.

Return to Marsden for the night.

Retrace your steps to The Reindeer. There is nowhere to stand on the opposite side of the road for the return bus so wait on the pub side, watch for the bus to come from the left and wave it down.

Bus 232 d. The Reindeer for Huddersfield bus stn. Mo-Su 1/hr

Bus 184, 350, 351, 352 d. Huddersfield bus stn for Marsden Mo-Sa 5/hr; Su every 2/hr (31 min)

MetroTrain d. Huddersfield for Marsden Mo-Sa 1/hr; Su every 2 hr (13 min)

Yorkshire Sculpture Park (YSP)

Open daily. Grounds 10.00-18.00
Shop and Restaurant 10.00-17.00
Galleries 11.00-17.00 (16.00 for Longfield Gallery)
Cost: free
Tel. 01924 832 631
W: www.ysp.co.uk

GETTING THERE
Bus 231 d. Huddersfield bus station for West Bretton Mo-Sa 1/hr No Su service. Ask to be let off for the Sculpture Park, which is also known as Leeds University West Bretton campus. (30 min)

On alighting continue down the road to the T-junction. Turn left, then right at the cenotaph. The park is at the end of the road. (6 min walk)

Within the park the road diverges. The left branch leads to the visitor centre, food, shop and indoor galleries. Follow the left branch until you see a broad flight of steps on the left. Climb the steps and turn left onto a gravel path that leads to a long modern building. To avoid climbing the long flight of steps that now confront you keep to the right of the building and walk to the far end where the lift is cunningly hidden. Being a split-level building there are two ground floors: GL has the café, G and 1 have the galleries.

The YSP covers 500 acres of sculpture-strewn 18thC parkland. Changing exhibitions are held inside the gallery.

There is a restaurant and coffee shop in the visitor centre and an ice cream/cold drinks kiosk in the park.

The YSP is not luggage-friendly at all! Sign-posting is poor and the visitor centre is hidden from view to those arriving by bus. Worse, it is up a long flight of steps or via an artfully hidden lift

that opens onto empty echoing corridors devoid of life or hope or even helpful signs. I strongly recommend visiting it unencumbered! Having said that, I do recommend a visit if modern art appeals. The setting is pleasing and the sculptures are, for the most part, easily visible.

RETURN to MARSDEN
Bus 231 d. West Bretton for Huddersfield bus stn. Mo-Sa 1/hr. No Su service. Stop is on opposite side of road from where alighted.

Bus 184, 350, 351, 352 d. Huddersfield bus stn for Marsden Mo-Sa 5/hr; Su every 2/hr (31 min)

MetroTrain d. Huddersfield for Marsden Mo-Sa 1/hr; Su every 2 hr (13 min)

Getting Home

From Huddersfield there are frequent trains to Leeds and from Leeds there are mainline trains to just about everywhere.

Highlights of Tour 4

- Mainline Rail Station: Newcastle
  - Two nights in Tynemouth
    - Days 1 & 2 – castle and priory, Segedunum, Arbeia, Beamish Open Air Museum, Gibside 18thC Park
    - Day 3 – travel to Hexham via Cherryburn or George Stephenson's Birthplace
  - Three or four nights in Hexham
    - Days 4, 5 – Hexham Cathedral, Hadrian's Wall and forts at Housesteads, Vindolanda and Chesters
  - Overnight in Alston or Hexham
    - Day 6 – Pennine side-trip or Birdoswald fort and/or Roman Army Museum
  - Overnight in Carlisle
    - Day 7 – Tullie House Museum, castle, cathedral
- Mainline Rail Station: Carlisle

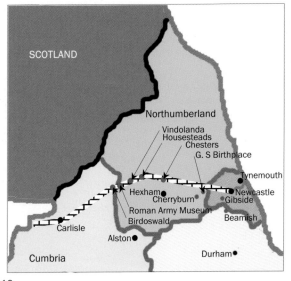

Tour 4 – Hadrian's Wall: Northumberland & Cumbria

Hadrian seems to have chosen the northern frontier of his empire with an eye to future generations of tourists. His famous wall swoops and tumbles with military precision and artistic sensibility across some of the most dramatic landscape in England's north country.

This tour follows Hadrian's Wall from the east coast to Carlisle, plunging the traveller into civilian and military Roman life. If that sounds a bit heavy, don't fret; the scenery is fabulous and there is a lot more up there than a wall! Read on.

Tynemouth is a classic seaside resort that serves as a base from which to visit the Roman forts of Arbeia across the river in South Shields and Segedunum at Wallsend. For variety there are the North of England Open Air Museum at Beamish and an 18thC park at Gibside, which is dotted with stables, follies, orangery and Palladian chapel.

Next is the cathedral and market town of Hexham. By bus from Newcastle you can break the journey at Mickley Square to visit Cherryburn, the farm that was the birthplace of artist and naturalist Thomas Bewick. The train from Newcastle stops at Wylam, where a gentle half-mile walk takes you to the tiny cottage where George Stephenson was born.

Hexham is handily located for the Roman forts at Housesteads, Vindolanda, Chesters and Birdoswald. The most photographed section of the wall starts at Housesteads, so plan for a wild and windy hike that is manageable for anyone sound in wind and limb.

A detour south climbs to the highest market town in England: Alston. In wet, foggy weather give it a miss; on a clear day the drive is spectacular. Alston provides Pennine walks, art galleries, craft shops and the South Tynedale Railway.

Finally, Carlisle. The Roman exhibition in the Tullie House museum will round off your campaign very nicely, while the castle and cathedral will add variety to your historical diet.

Accommodation (see page 10 for abbreviations)

TYNEMOUTH, Tyne & Wear – 2 nights
No. 61 Guest House, 61 Front Street, Tynemouth NE30 4BT
Tel. 0191 257 3687
Rooms (£/room) 2Te (£55-£60); 3De (£55-£65); 2Fe (£65+);
S in D £40

Martineau Guest House, 57 Front Street, Tynemouth NE30 4BX
Tel. 0191 296 0746
E:martineau.house@ukgateway.net   W: www.martineau-house.co.uk
Rooms (£/room) 1Te/De, 2De (£65); S in Te/De £45-£55
No children under 14

Holford Guest House, 36 Beverley Terrace, Cullercoats NE30 4NU
Tel. 0191 252 8718; E: admpholford@aol.com
Rooms (£/room): 6Ss (£22.50); 2Ts, 2Ds (£43-£47); 2Fs (£43-£50)
Cullercoats is one Metro stop on, or a few minutes' walk along the
sandy beach from Tynemouth.

Failing the above, there are many places to stay in Whitley Bay, one
Metro stop on from Cullercoats. TIC Whitley Bay Tel. 0191 200 8535
or E: ticwb@northtyneside.gov.uk

HEXHAM, Northumberland – 3 nights
Station Inn, Station Road, Hexham NE46 1EZ
Tel: 01434 603 155
E: info@stationinnhexham.co.uk   W: ww.stationinnhexham.co.uk
Rooms(£/room) 2Se (£30); 5Te, 1De (£50); 1Fe (£75)

West Close House, Hextol Terrace, Hexham NE46 2AD
Tel. 01434 603 307
Rooms (£pppn): 2Ss (£21-£24), 2De (£23-£30). No children.

Queensgate House, Cockshaw, Hexham NE46 3QU
Tel. 01434 605 592
Rooms (£/room) 1 Ss (£19); 1Se (£25); 1Te (£40); 1Ds (£38);
1Fe (£45)

ALSTON, Cumbria – 1 night
Victoria Inn, Front Street, Alston CA9 3SE
Tel. 01434 381 194; E: victoriainncumbria@talk21.com
Rooms (£pppn) 3Ss (£20); 1Se (£25); 1Ds (£17.50); 1De (£20);
1Fs (£17.50); 1Fe (£20)

Cumberland Hotel, Townfoot, Alston CA9 3HX
Tel. 01434 381 875
E: HelenGuyH@aol.com   W: www.alstoncumberlandhotel.co.uk
Rooms (£pppn) 2Te, 2De, 1Fe (£26); S in T/D £31

YHA, The Firs, Alston CA9 3RW
Tel. 0870 770 5668; Int (+44) 1434 381 509; E: alston@yha.org.uk
Cost: £11.00/£8.00
Open Apr-Jun, Sep, Oct flexible; Jul, Aug daily
Rec. 8.00-10.00; 17.00-22.00
No family rooms, no under 3s, no cot

CARLISLE, Cumbria – 1 night
YHA, Old Brewery Residences, Bridge Lane, Caldewgate,
Carlisle CA2 5SR
Tel. 0870 770 5752; Int (+44) 1228 597 352
E: deec@impacthousing.org.uk
Cost: £16.00/£12.00
Note: University Residence, open daily Jul & Aug only
Rec. 8.00-10.00; 17.00 - 22.00
Single bedrooms in flats for up to 7 people. Self-catering. Laundry.

Craighead, 6 Hartington Place, Carlisle CA1 1HL
Tel. 01228 596 767
Rooms (£pppn) 1Ss (£21); 1Ts, 1Ds (£19-£20); 1De (£23)
1Fs (£19-£20 + children) No children under 3 yrs.

Howard House, 27 Howard Place, Carlisle CA1 1HR
Tel: 01228 529 159; E: howardhouse@bigfoot.com
Rooms (£pppn): 2Ss (£18); 1Ts, 1Ds (£20): 1Se, 1Te, 1De (£25)
No children under 6 yrs.

Historical Background

They came. They saw…

Julius Caesar's expeditions to Britain in 55BC and 54BC resulted in trade with the Britons but not their absorption into the Roman empire. That was to begin around AD43 with the unexpected rise of Claudius to emperor of Rome and his desire for overseas conquest.

They conquered – almost

The occupation of Britain began in the south. By the time Gnaeus Julius Agricola arrived in AD74, Romanisation had spread sufficiently to enable him to develop a network of forts across the north. Soon the legions were ready to march into Scotland.

However, although forts and roads were built up to the rivers Forth and Clyde, the Scottish tribes proved more trouble than the land was worth: in AD118 the entire Ninth Legion disappeared, presumably slaughtered by the Scots and Picts. The Romans withdrew to the Stanegate, a road between Carlisle and Corbridge.

The Wall

In AD122 the emperor Hadrian visited Britain and decided to define the northern boundary by a wall from Segedunum, about four miles up the Tyne from the coast, to the Solway Firth.

Initially the Wall was a turf and timber embankment with milecastles interspersed with turrets and supplemented by existing forts a bit south along the Stanegate. Later the timber was replaced by stone and eleven forts were added along the Wall itself.

The Wall started nine and a half feet thick, but, as building material ran low, the thickness was reduced to seven and a half feet. A platform for patrols, protected by battlements on the north edge, ran along the top. Invaders from the north would face a ditch thirty feet

They came   ©LEGIIAVG

wide and ten feet deep, then the sheer 21.5-foot height of the wall.

The fortifications

At every Roman mile (about nine-tenths of a modern mile) there was a milecastle with a fortified gate tower and two barrack houses, all within a walled enclosure.

Equally spaced between these milecastles were two turrets, each with a hearth and stores on the ground floor and a ladder leading up to the first floor guardroom. The turrets were manned by soldiers from the milecastles.

The forts were rectangular and surrounded by a round-cornered wall and a ditch. The wall was stone or turf and timber, banked on the inside by earth. Ovens, latrines and workshops were built against the embankment. Within the confines of the walls were long rectangular barracks, granaries, storehouses and stables.

Immediately south of the Wall was the military road (not to be confused with the Stanegate), which can still be traced.

The entire military zone of Wall, forts and road was protected on the south by a vallum: a ten-foot deep ditch, twenty feet wide at the top, flanked to the north and south by ten-foot high earth embankments.

The legions guarding the Wall were a combination of infantry and cavalry. Since Romans were notoriously bad horsemen, the cavalry units were auxiliaries: soldiers from Roman territories who were not yet citizens.

Hadrian's successor moved troops 100 miles north and in 142 erected the Antonine Wall between the rivers Forth and Clyde.

From 208 to 210 there were more campaigns in Scotland. These were unsuccessful, on the whole, and the Romans retreated to the south of Hadrian's Wall for good in 211.

They left

Early in the fifth century the legions in Britain were recalled to

Hadrian's Wall near Housesteads

defend Rome against invading Goths. Many of the Wall forts remained occupied into the sixth century, but there was a general decline in maintenance and living standards.

The Wall provided a seemingly endless supply of dressed stone that could not be ignored. Bits of Hadrian's Wall are to be found in northern churches, houses and field walls.

Roman forts in the care of English Heritage have excellent illustrated information boards at strategic locations around the sites.

Days 1 and 2 – In and Around Tynemouth

The long expanses of sandy beach at Tynemouth let you enjoy a taste of the traditional English seaside holiday within easy reach by Metro and bus of Segedunum, Arbeia, Beamish and Gibside.

The town sits on the north side the Tyne estuary. While it cannot boast a Roman fort, fragments of pottery suggest a Roman settlement of some sort where the ruins of a castle and priory stand on a high promontory.

Main line railway station:
NEWCASTLE

GETTING to TYNEMOUTH
From Newcastle rail stn take the Metro to Tynemouth. The Metro entrance is within Newcastle Central railway station; look for the black M on a yellow square. Buy your ticket from one of the machines before reaching the platforms.
Choose the platform and train that goes to St. James via Whitley Bay (not the airport train, which leaves from the same platform). Electronic signs above the platform indicate when the next train is due and its destination. A sign on the train also gives the destination.

Tynemouth's Promontory
The south shore of the Tyne estuary holds the better defensive position, but Tynemouth's promontory provides the better view of the coast. The rocky platform, surrounded by water on three sides and a massive trench on the landward side, has served concurrent multiple purposes for close to 1,400 years.

There is evidence of the Anglo-Saxon monastery where King (later Saint) Oswin of Deira (roughly what is now Yorkshire), who was killed by his cousin King (later Saint) Oswy of Northumbria, was buried in 651.

The monastery was destroyed by Vikings in the ninth century but rose again as a Benedictine priory after the Norman Conquest. For protection against Scottish invaders, the priory was within the bailey of the new Norman castle.

The priory church tower doubled as a lighthouse until the seventeenth century, and the present Coastguard regional headquarters are adjacent to the priory ruins.

The priory was dissolved by Henry VIII in 1539 and the site incorporated into his coastal defence network. Twentieth century gun batteries are still in place overlooking the sea.

Tynemouth Priory & Castle (EH)

Open daily Apr-Sep 10.00-18.00
Oct 10.00-16.00
Cost: A £3.30/Co £2.50/Ch £1.70
Tel. 0191 257 1090

The Priory

The ruins we see today are the remains of the Norman Benedictine priory founded in 1085 by monks from St. Albans Abbey in Hertfordshire. Durham would have been the obvious choice of mother house for the Norman monastery, as it had been for the Anglo-Saxon, but the Earl of Northumberland had argued with the Bishop of Durham and awarded the site to the southern abbey, which later sent its unruly monks to exile in Tynemouth!

The remains of St. Oswin were moved from the still-standing Anglo-Saxon church to a shrine behind the altar of the new Norman church. The nave was used as the church for the parish, which had its own vicar. See pages 46 and 47 for more on monasteries and churches.

The monastery could hardly have been described as a haven of peace, prayer and learning. Perhaps the exiled unruly monks liked to stir up trouble, or the priory just became too rich and ambitious for its own good: it owned land and coal deposits and established the town of North Shields. Whatever the reason, the priory was not locally popular. In 1270 the mayor of Newcastle led an army of volunteers to attack North Shields, burn its mills and steal a load of coal. In 1294 the abbot of St. Albans joined forces with the mayor of Newcastle to forcibly remove the prior of Tynemouth.

The priory was used as a royal guest house for kings Edward II, Edward III and Richard II. That didn't save it from the wrath of Henry VIII and it was dissolved in 1539.

The church was allowed to remain for the benefit of the parish, and its tower continued its role as a lighthouse.

By the Restoration of Charles II

in 1660, the church was in ruins. It was replaced by a new church in North Shields.

For more on monasteries and their dissolution, see pages 46, 47 and 57.

The Castle

The original timber motte and bailey castle (see page 61 for more on castles) belonged to Robert de Mowbray, the same Earl of Northumberland who argued with the bishop of Durham. When de Mowbray rebelled against William Rufus, successor to William the Conqueror, the castle withstood a two-month siege, but de Mowbray was eventually captured, imprisoned and sent to St. Albans monastery where he died.

Because the priory was built within the bailey it was obliged to maintain the castle and garrison. In 1346 the prior was awarded sole authority within the fortified walls, and Tynemouth was soon described as one of the strongest fortresses along the Scottish border. It was about this time that the existing gatehouse was built. It may have served as the guest house for visiting dignitaries.

The site was refortified as part of Henry VIII's coastal defences. The garrison was housed in the priory buildings, but, to be effective, the gun batteries had to be placed at a lower level on the southern face of the promontory.

The castle changed hands several times during the Civil War and by the Restoration it was in ruins. The governor built a lighthouse to replace the one on the church tower, which had served since Norman times.

From the early eighteenth century, repairs and modifications continued on the castle in response to changing armaments and enemies. The castle remained operational to the end of World War II and continued in the hands of the military until 1960.

The site has been in the care of English Heritage since 1984.

Around Tynemouth

If you are obsessed with Roman history you may want to visit both Segedunum and Arbeia; otherwise, choose one then head out to Beamish for the North of England Open Air Museum or to Rowlands Gill for Gibside, your only opportunity on this tour to visit, if not a stately home, then at least a stately park.

The actual remains of the Roman forts at both Segedunum and Arbeia cover a great deal of ground but are mostly no more than a few inches high. Far more impressive remains will be seen from Hexham. **Segedunum** has a comprehensive museum that is a good introduction to the Roman occupation of Britain and to Hadrian's Wall. The site also boasts a full-scale replica of a bath house. The attraction is only five-minutes' walk from the Metro.

Arbeia has a smaller museum but offers full-scale replicas of a gatehouse, barracks and villa. South Shields is a seaside town, which Wallsend is not, but the attraction is about twenty-minutes' walk, much of it uphill, from the Metro.

In either case, if you decide to go to Beamish aim to leave no later than 11.30 to enjoy a good four hours' visit.

Segedunum
Open daily Apr-Aug 9.30-17.30
Sep-Oct 10:00-17.00
Cost: A £3.50/CoCh £1.95
EH members 10% discount
Tel. 0191 236 9347
www.twmuseums.org.uk/segedunum

GETTING THERE
Take the Metro to Wallsend. Exit in the direction away from the bus stn, turn right into the main road towards Swan & Hunter shipbuilders and right again into Buddle Street (the major intersection before Swan & Hunter). Segedunum is on the far right-hand corner, a 5-min walk from the Metro. Signposting is good.

The museum contains tableaux, interactive displays, a film and games, all demonstrating life in and around a Northumbrian Roman fort. Underneath the entertaining froth there is a great deal of solid information.

An Industrial Gallery relates the coal and shipbuilding history of Wallsend.

The much-vaunted tower, designed to blend with the Swan & Hunter ship-building yard, provides a panoramic view of the foundations of the fort. Apart from the magnitude of the site, the view is anticlimactic.

The reconstructed and fully functional (when not damaged by vandals) Bath House is open at regular intervals throughout the day. Functional or not, its size, décor and complexity are fascinating.

Metro te Saluere Iubert
In prouincia Tineae et Vedrae Nemo viatores melius adiuuat

Itineris Tessera tibi emenda est antequam in uehiculum ineas.

Dum apud Metronem es Tessera tibi sic retinenda est ut inspici possit. Consilium Vectura Poenali multandi habemus.

Wallsend Metro Station

Arbeia Roman Fort & Museum

Open Easter-Sep Mo-Sa 10.00-17.30; Su 13.00-17.00
Oct-Easter Mo-Sa 10.00-16.00; Su closed
Cost: free
Tel. 0191 456 1369
W: www.twmuseums.org.uk/Arbeia

GETTING THERE
From Wallsend or Tynemouth take the Metro to North Shields, then walk (10 min) or take the connecting bus to the ferry landing. Cross the Tyne on the ferry to South Shields.

From South Shields ferry landing follow the signs to the Metro, then keep walking until you reach the end of the pedestrian precinct near the busy intersection with Anderson Street. Cross Anderson, continue on Ocean Road and turn left into Baring Street (first left after Anderson).

Keep walking for about 10 min until you see the single storey red brick museum to the right.

Arbeia was a supply base and garrison. The emphasis on each role depended on the times.

Arbeia, which means "the place of the Arabs", was probably so named by the Tigris bargemen who were the last troops to garrison the fort.

Arbeia remained inhabited some time after the Roman troops left, and Oswin, King of Deira, was born there. However, in common with many others, the fort was eventually abandoned.

The small museum building contains material from the fort, the surrounding civilian settlement and the cemetery. The reconstructed West Gate is mildly interesting; the barracks, where you can see the living conditions of a soldier, centurion and commanding officer, are more so. All too easy to miss, especially if there is filming going on, is the reconstructed courtyard house behind the barracks. There are several furnished rooms and bright frescos on the walls. On the whole, a visit to Arbeia is probably worth the extra effort.

Beamish – The North of England Open Air Museum

Open daily 10.00-17.00
Cost: A £15.00/Co £12.00/Ch £9.00 Show your bus ticket and save £4.00
Tel. 0191 370 4000
W: www.beamish.org.uk

GETTING THERE
Take the Metro to Gateshead. From Tynemouth and Wallsend change at Monument for the yellow or green line. From South Shields the green line is direct.

At Gateshead follow the bus signs that point straight ahead from the turnstile. When you get to the street, but still within the building, go up the steps or escalator on your right and you will be in Gateshead Interchange. An electronic departures board ahead on your right directs you to the correct platform.

Bus 709 d. Gateshead Interchange for Beamish Mo-Sa 1/hr; Su/BH 2/hr (37 min).

Within the 300 acres of the museum lie a 1913 railway station, farm, town and colliery village. From 1825 are the house, gardens and stables of a yeoman farmer, and the Pockerley Waggonway.

A bonus of the trip is seeing the metal statue, The Angel of the North, created by Antony Gormley OBE. Look to your right about ten minutes after leaving the Gateshead bus station.

After exploring the mine, drop by the pit cottages. The villagers will show you how to make lace out of newspaper and how to turn a baby chair into a walker and a rocker. Practice your handwriting on the slates at the school then catch a tram to town to fuel up at the sweetie shop. Enjoy a picnic on the green, have a go on the Merry-go-round, then head off to see the historic breeds of horses, cows, sheep, ducks and hens at the Home Farm and Pockerley Manor.

There is plenty more to see, as well as a range of refreshments at the tea room, coffee shop and pub, so allow anywhere from three to five hours for your visit.

RETURN to TYNEMOUTH
Allow 10 to 15 min to walk from the entrance building uphill to the bus stop. When you reach the road, turn left and walk past the Shepherd & Shepherdess pub. The bus stop is clearly indicated. Bus 709 d. Beamish Mo-Sa 1/hr, Su/BH 2/hour (37 min).

Gibside (NT)
Open daily Grounds 10.00-18.00
Chapel & Stables 11.00-16.30
Shop & Tea-room 11.00-17.00
Cost: A £3.50/Ch £2.00
Tel. 01207 541820
E: gibside@nationaltrust.org.uk

GETTING THERE
Take Metro to Central Station. Buses 45, 46, 46A, 47, 47A leave outside Central Station for Rowlands Gill Mo-Sa 6/hr; Su 4/hr (33 min) The bus stops near the start of Rowlands Gill. Turn left and follow the road down to the river and over the bridge. Turn left again through the gates to Gibside. The ½-mile route is sign-posted.

"Designed landscape" is the best way to describe the 18thC park at Gibside. It is much more than a garden or even what one might think of as a park.

The Long Walk, for example, is a straight half-mile of grass bordered by trees. It's enough to make one itch for a gallop, and the creator of it all, George Bowes, did just that with his race horses.

Artistically distributed around the parkland, woods and hills are a Palladian chapel (topped by what appears to be a wedding cake under a scanty parasol), a towering Column to Liberty, a functional stable courtyard, fairy-castle banqueting house, an orangery and the shell of a Jacobean mansion.

There are waymarked walks and a tea room.

Another interesting attraction in the area is **Bede's World**. For more information see page 43.

Day 3 – Tynemouth to Hexham

Having sampled a fort or two, and refreshed your memory of Roman history, you are ready to tackle the Wall in earnest. It is 73 miles long, but the best bits are within easy reach of Hexham.

There are two interesting National Trust properties en route to Hexham: George Stephenson's birthplace and Cherryburn. Both are small, but each is located in attractive countryside a short walk from the train or bus stop. A pleasant light lunch is available at both.

For a visit to George Stephenson's birthplace take the train to Hexham via Wylam. For a visit to Cherryburn, take the bus via Mickley Square.

GETTING to HEXHAM via WYLAM
Take the Metro to Newcastle Central Station. Train d. Newcastle for

Hexham or Carlisle via Wylam Mo-Su 1/hr (15 min)

NOTE: Generally, trains that terminate at Hexham stop at Wylam. Many trains to Carlisle do *not* stop at Wylam.

At Wylam cross the tracks and follow the road over the bridge. Continue to the right of the village green and on to the path with the car park on your right (more or less a straight line from the rail station).

On the far side of the car park turn right (signposted) and follow the level cinder bicycle path about ½ mile. Within 10-15 min of leaving the station you will see a white cottage with a large commemorative plaque on your left.

Take the same train from the same platform to continue to Hexham (22 min)

George Stephenson's Birthplace (NT)

Open Th-Su/BH 12.00-17.00
Cost: A £1.00/Ch 50p
Tel. 01661 853457

George Stephenson was born in this cottage in 1781 and lived for eight years with his parents and four siblings in the one room that is now open to the public.

Birthplace of George Stephenson

George started work at a mine, picking debris from the coal. He was upgraded to horse driver when he was ten and by seventeen was in charge of a pumping engine keeping water out of the pits. At eighteen he began learning to read and by 22 he was a father – of Robert Stephenson.

By working his way through the ranks and gaining increasing responsibility for the engines at the coal mines, George could afford to send Robert to school.

George Stephenson is best known for his work on the railways, transforming the early, heavy steam locomotives of Trevithick into more efficient machines for hauling freight and passengers reliably and safely. He planned and oversaw the building of the Stockton and Darlington Railway, the first steam locomotive-powered passenger railway in the world.

Robert Stephenson was a close partner in this and together they worked on the *Rocket*, which was built under Robert's direction.

Robert is best known for his bridges: the High Level Bridge in Newcastle and the Royal Border Bridge at Berwick-upon-Tweed.

In the room will be a costumed and well-informed volunteer to fill in all the details of Stephenson's life and times. It may not sound like much, but Stephenson's birthplace generates a vivid glimpse into the lives and changing fortunes of a lower working class family from 1781.

Access is by foot, horse or bicycle, so it is a very peaceful and enjoyable walk.

GOOD EATING

A tea room is tucked behind the whitewashed stone cottage. In this idyllic setting you can enjoy a light lunch with locally baked cakes.

GETTING to HEXHAM via MICKLEY SQUARE

Take the Metro to Newcastle Central Station. Exit the railway station by following the signs for Taxis. Outside, turn left and walk down the line of bus stops. The stop for Bus 602 is near the far end.

Bus 602 d. Newcastle Central Station Mo-Sa 2/hr; Su/BH 1/hr (50 min). Ask for a Day Rover ticket and to be let off at Mickley Square outside The Jiggery-Pokery Tea Room.

Across the road is a brown sign pointing to Cherryburn, which is an easy 5-min downhill walk.

Pick up the same bus from the same stop to continue to Hexham (25 min)

Cherryburn (NT)

Open Th-Tu 11.00-17.00
Cost: A £3.50/Ch £1.75
Tel. 01661 843 276
E: cherryburn@nationaltrust.org.uk

One room of a 19thC stone farmhouse displays illustrations by artist, naturalist and wood engraver Thomas Bewick. His work includes a catalogue of English Birds, another of Quadrupeds and some illustrated editions of selected Aesop's Fables. Several stuffed Birds and Quadrupeds (little ones) are mounted next to their respective prints.

Behind the house, enjoying the fine views of the Tyne valley, you will find donkey sisters Henrietta and Esmerelda. *Please* do not feed them, as they are well fed and may get very sick if given the wrong thing.

Adjacent to the donkey shed is a two-room cottage furnished as it would have been in 1753 when Bewick was born there. The Bewick family later moved into the farmhouse that contains the exhibition.

Take time to explore the garden in front of the house. The paths lead to all sorts of hidden delights behind the hedges.

Special events are held every Sunday afternoon from April through October between 13.00 and 16.30. These include press room demonstrations using traditional methods on original hand presses, and *Folk in the Farmyard*, amateur and professional performers of traditional music, folk song and country dance.

GOOD EATING

I suggest visiting Cherryburn, then recovering from the uphill climb back to the bus stop by having lunch at *The Jiggery Pokery Tea Room*. You can get freshly baked hot or cold sandwiches, quiches, omelettes and salads, as well as a variety of cakes, pies and biscuits. The food is delicious and the price reasonable.

Note: The owner retired two days after my visit, but the pastry cook stayed on.

Hexham

Within Hexham itself, the cathedral is the thing to visit, especially since it houses one of the finest Roman tombstones you are ever likely to see.

The building of Hexham Cathedral began around 672 when the Anglo-Saxon Queen Etheldreda gave the land to the troublesome priest (later Saint) Wilfrid. For more on Wilfrid and Etheldreda, see pages 55 and 56.

All that remains of Wilfrid's church is the crypt, which was built using stone from the Roman fort at Corbridge. The rest was most likely destroyed by Viking raids in the eighth and ninth centuries.

After the Norman conquest a group of Augustinian canons was sent to Hexham to build a priory. They gradually rebuilt the Anglo-Saxon church on a grand scale.

One of the first things you see on entering the cathedral is the 13thC night stair used by the canons to descend from their dormitory to the church for the night services. The stair survived Henry VIII's dissolution of the priory in 1537.

At the foot of the stair is the

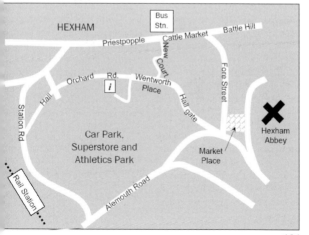

tombstone to Flavinus, the standard bearer of the Gaulish auxiliary cavalry regiment called the *Ala Petriana*. He and his horse are shown in full regalia with the soldier kicking a Celt in the posterior. Flavinus died towards the end of the first century at the age of 25, terminating seven years of military service. Exactly when and why his memorial was carried three miles from Corbridge, the nearest Roman cemetery, to a Christian church is something of a mystery, but its place of prominence is due to the Victorian archaeologist who found it.

Border History Museum

Open daily 10.00-16.30
Cost: A £3.00/CoCh £2.00
Tel. 01434 652 349

The museum is located in the first purpose-built gaol in England. Built in 1330 to imprison convicted reivers, it is logical that it concentrates on reiver history. For more on the reivers, see page 142.

Day 4 – Housesteads and Vindolanda

It is doubtful you will be able, or indeed willing, to see all the forts and museums along Hadrian's Wall. This brief assessment of the major attractions is intended to help you plan the next couple of days.

Chesters has the best fort and, although children may not think so, a fascinating museum.

Housesteads has a great location, the best stretch of wall and the best communal toilets (Roman, not twenty-first century!).

Vindolanda fort is too large and complex for the average visitor to form a really coherent picture of what is was like, especially since it is mostly foundations with very few walls. However, the museum, with indoor and outdoor re-

constructions, is great. Vindolanda is a 20 to 25 minute walk from the bus stop unless you take bus AD122 (see below).

Birdoswald fort isn't much and the Roman part of the museum adds nothing new, but the story of the Border Reivers is fascinating.

The **Roman Army Museum** is good, but not sufficiently different from museums at Segedunum and Carlisle to make it worth a special effort.

Hadrian's Wall Bus AD122

Bus AD122 runs to all the sites five times/day each way between Hexham and Carlisle (Easter week and mid-May to late September Mo-Su; April, early May, late September and October on Su/BH only).

One- or four-day Explorer tick

ets for unlimited travel on Bus AD122 are sold on the buses. Pick up the timetable from the TIC in Hexham.

Buses 185, 880 and 681

Chesters, Housesteads, the Roman Army Museum and Vindolanda are all accessible by bus from Hexham or Haltwhistle (19 minutes by train from Hexham) Monday to Saturday. On Sunday, take bus AD122.

The itinerary and the GETTING THERE information for the next two days are based on using Buses 185, 880 and 681, but remember that all sites are also reached by Bus AD122 on the days it operates.

Note that on Day 5 you must be back at Hexham bus station in time to catch the bus to Alston.

Housesteads Fort (EH & NT)

Open daily Apr-Sep 10.00-18.00
Oct 10.00-16.00
Cost: A £3.60/Co £2.70/Ch £1.80
Tel. 01434 344363

GETTING THERE
Train d. Hexham for Haltwhistle Mo-Su 1/hr (20 min). Cross the footbridge, exit the station and walk about 50 yards to the bus stop. Bus 185/681 d. Haltwhistle for Housesteads Fort Mo-Sa 4/day, first in late a.m. (16 min).

Roman-British home life   ©LEGIIAVG

The drive into the hills is very scenic. *Motion Sickness Alert!*

It is a steep uphill half-mile walk from the bus stop to the admission gate, shop, small museum and fort. Drinks, chocolate and sandwiches are sold at the National Trust booth in the car park – not at the shop. Get your supplies before heading uphill!

Once at the museum, take a few minutes to orient yourself with the scale model of the fort, which is extensive.

Particularly note-worthy is the seventeen-seater latrine where a stream of water cleared the waste and another cleaned the bottom-wiping sponges.

WALKING THE WALL:
HOUSESTEADS to HOTBANK
FARM
This 1½-mile walk follows the most scenically dramatic stretch of Hadrian's wall.

The path is well-used but rough and steep in places. If you are sound in wind and limb and wear hiking boots or strong shoes, you should have no problem, but do not underestimate the terrain or the variability and nastiness of the weather. See Tips for Safe Hiking on page 183.

As you leave Housesteads Fort, instead of following the path back to the museum, head diagonally across the field to your right to the sign post and stile. Then just keep the wall on your right. The hills are steep, but the views are good, especially back along the wall.

Hotbank Farm is the bleak farmyard on the north side of the wall. A mud track leads from the farm parallel to the wall, then turns left and intersects your path. Follow the track down to the B6318 (the main road back to Housesteads). At the main road turn right and walk about 500 yards to pick up a footpath on the south side of the road. This footpath will lead you to Vindolanda. Refer to Ordnance Survey Outdoor Leisure Map 43.

Vindolanda

Open daily Apr–Sep 10.00–17.00
Oct 10.00-16.00
Cost: A £4.50/Co £3.80/Ch £2.90
EH members 10% discount
Tel. 01434 344 277
W: www.vindolanda.com

GETTING THERE
If you prefer not to walk the Wall, catch Bus185/681 from Housesteads car park and get off at Once Brewed Youth Hostel (5 min) Follow the minor road (signposted for Vindolanda) past the National Park Visitor Centre. Turn left into the single lane road (also sign-posted) and keep walking for about 1½ miles from the Youth Hostel. Allow 30 min

Vindolanda was built on the Stanegate about forty years before the building of Hadrian's Wall. The early forts were of wood and required periodic rebuilding. Before each rebuild the previous remains were smoothed-over with clay and turf, which preserved artefacts that would otherwise have decomposed.

The visible remains are of the stone fort. Excavations continue Sunday to Friday, April to August, weather permitting.

The museum is beautifully located in a wooded valley with an ornamental pond and stream. Here, with a modicum of imagination, the Roman world comes to life.

A large civilian settlement developed outside the fort walls and from that come elegant ladies' sandals, tiny children's shoes and sturdy soldiers' boots; beads, brooches and bracelets, woven baskets, cloth and painted glassware. Life around a Roman garrison in the wild northern tip of the empire was not totally uncivilised.

The ratty bits of wood in the next room are the most precious treasure of Vindolanda: the earliest written records from Britain preserved for close to 2,000 years in the clay under the fort. They include military and personal letters, accounts and records.

The small open air museum clusters around the pond: a Roman home, shop, temple to the Nymphs and garden, as well as a 17thC stone croft. Press the buttons to hear voice from the past.

GETTING BACK TO HEXHAM

From Vindolanda car park follow the lane heading to your left.

Look out on your right for Causeway House, an18thC heather and turf-thatched farmhouse. No access to interior.

Turn right at the intersection with the slightly wider road, continue to the B6318 at Once Brewed and turn left. Wait by the wall of the Youth Hostel parking lot next to the main road (there is no bus stop sign).

GOOD to KNOW

The Once Brewed National Park Visitor Centre has ice cream, cold drinks and toilets.

Day 5 – Half-day at Chesters

After visiting Chesters there is time to explore Hexham more thoroughly before continuing to the Pennine town of Alston. If the weather is set to be wet and misty you may prefer to stay another night in Hexham to visit Birdoswald and the Roman Army Museum on Day 6.

Chesters Roman Fort (EH)

Open daily Apr-Sep 9.30-18.00
Oct 10.00-16.00
Cost: A £3.60/Co £2.70/Ch £1.80
Tel. 01434 681 379

GETTING THERE
Bus 880 d. Hexham bus stn for Chollerford Mo-Sa at erratic intervals of about 1-2 hr; Su/BH 3/day (15 min) Ask for Chesters and alight just after the roundabout at Chollerford. Walk back to the roundabout and turn right (see map). Chesters Roman Fort is a flat ¼ mile from bus stop.

The museum

The cramped two-room museum is much as it was when it was built for the collection of John Clayton, an Edwardian lawyer who was dedicated to preserving and excavating Roman remains along the Wall.

On first sight the collection looks decidedly dull – shelf upon shelf of inscribed stones and a few display cases of odds and ends.

But take a closer look: there are sculptures of gods and nymphs, carved heads of all sorts, gravestone eulogies and much more.

Take the time to read the translations and you will soon start to recognise some of the cohorts and may even take a friendly interest in their activities and well-being.

The odds and ends in the display cases are household items that really give life to the long-dead soldiers and their families. They include some beautifully iridescent fragments of glass and the Chesters Terrier – a fine little dog.

In the second room are paintings of Roman soldiers reconstructed from gravestones within the museum and elsewhere. Flavinus of Hexham Cathedral makes an appearance. This little museum is really quite a treasure chest.

The fort

The compact layout and the height of many of the walls make it easy to visualise Chesters Fort in its original state. You can walk around and explore everywhere – even inside the strong room.

The bath house by the river must have heard some colourful language as freshly bathed soldiers emerged from its warmth to face he wet and windy run back to their barracks. That their commanding officer's house was centrally heated and their barracks were not must have been a sore point!

You will have about 2¼ hours between buses to see the museum and the fort. Make sure you wait at the correct bus stop for the return journey (see map below).

GOOD EATING

The tea room between the fort and the museum offers sandwiches, cakes and hot and cold drinks. A snug little haven for warming up or cooling off.

RETURN TO HEXHAM

Bus 880 d. outside The George (see map below) for Hexham bus station (18 min).

GETTING TO ALSTON

Bus 888 Alston d. Hexham bus stn Mo-Sa in the early evening. No Su service except Jul-Sep 1/day in a.m. (50 min)

Major Motion Sickness Alert!

There are hairpin bends as well as gentler curves and all too numerous dips. The route, which at first runs through woods and beside rivers, climbs into the Pennines, an area far more barren than around Housesteads.

Bus stops near Chesters Fort

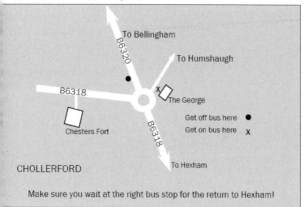

Make sure you wait at the right bus stop for the return to Hexham!

Day 6 – Option: Alston & North Pennines

The highest market town in England, Alston has cobbled streets, stone houses, hidden alleys and pretty gardens. The market cross, half-way down the steep main street, has twice been hit by runaway lorries but the benches under it's roof are still favoured places to sit.

The market square is surrounded by a variety of 19thC buildings housing shops, cafés and pubs. Although art and craft shops are creeping in, Alston retains it's market-town character.

You can easily spend the day pottering around the galleries, enjoying a meal at one of the tea rooms or inns and walking by the river or into the Pennines.

The early 18thC clock and bell in Alston church were presented by the Commissioners of Greenwich Hospital, whose coat of arms is shown above.

South Tynedale Railway

Four or five trips every Sa, Su, BH and on seasonal weekdays
Cost: A £5.00/Ch £2.00 return to Kirkhaugh
Tel. 01434 381 696
W: www.strps.org.uk

England's highest narrow gauge railway runs between Alston and Kirkhaugh. The round trip takes one hour. There is no road access to Kirkhaugh, so it is a peaceful place to picnic and walk.

Alston Model Railway Centre

Open daily 11.00-17.00
Cost: A £1.75/Co £1.25/Ch 75p
Tel. 01434 382100
W: www.alstonmodelrailwaycentre. co.uk

This little museum is located in the Station Yards Workshop opposite the South Tynedale Railway. It features changing displays of operational model railways with a range of track gauges. Next door is a well-stocked model railway shop. This is not just about trains but about whole miniature worlds!

Walks Around Alston

From the market cross, walk down the lane beside the Turk's Head then follow the path by the river Nent to the Packhorse Bridge for a good view of the Seven Sisters Waterfall (fifteen minutes).

The TIC sells descriptive book

lets of Pennine walks. Ask for one with walks starting in Alston.

GOOD EATING

Blueberry's Tea Shop, located at the lower end of the market square, serves traditional meals – from sandwiches to Boozy Pie, ice cream to Sticky Ginger Pudding with custard – all at a moderate price.

GETTING TO CARLISLE
Bus 680 d. Alston for Carlisle, The Courts Mo-Fr 2/day, Sa 3/day. No Su service (55 min). The bus stop is opposite Henderson's Garage. This trip, still very scenic, is not as dramatic as the drive from Hexham but is still a *Motion Sickness Alert!*

Day 6 – Option: More of the Wall

There is something new to see and learn in every museum, but, unless you are very keen, your eyes may start to glaze over in the Roman Army Museum (RAM) and Birdoswald Roman Fort. They are included only for those people determined to gain maximum Roman exposure.

If Bus AD122 is running the travelling is easy, but if you are dependent on Bus 185 it becomes more complicated. The RAM is easily reached, but Birdoswald is 1¼ miles from the bus stop, the bus is infrequent and there may well be a long (as in an hour or so) wait for the train back to Hexham. Be sure you want to do this and remember, you don't *have* to do both!

Buses AD122 and 185 run directly to Carlisle. Remember your luggage if planning to visit one or both of these sites en route to Car-

lisle. Telephone ahead to verify left luggage policies at the attractions. Alternatively, return to Hexham for the night or to continue to Alston. Times given are for bus 185 only; use bus AD122 whenever possible.

The Roman Army Museum
Open daily Apr-Sep 10.00-18.00
Oct 10.00-17.00
Cost: A £3.50/Co £3.00/Ch £2.20
Tel. 016977 47485
W: www.vindolanda.com

GETTING THERE
Train d. Hexham for Haltwhistle Mo-Su 1/hr (19 min). At Haltwhistle cross the footbridge, exit the station and walk about 50 yard to the bus stop.
Bus 185 d. Haltwhistle for RAM Mo-Sa 4/day (9 min). The bus goes about 50 yards past the Museum entrance into the Walltown Quarry parking lot before stopping.

This museum offers the usual array of artefacts, models and interpretive pictures.

Given the emphasis on the museum's film *Eagle's Eye*, it may come as is a bit of a let-down: computer-generated effects are no longer a novelty. For me the best bits were the close-up shots of the eagle. The Roman Army recruiting film, however, is both interesting and entertaining.

Birdoswald Roman Fort (EH)
Open daily 10.00-17.30
Cost: A £3.60/Co £2.70/Ch £1.80
Tel. 01697 747 602
W: www.birdoswaldromanfort.org

GETTING THERE
Bus 185 d. RAM Mo-Sa 4/day and stops at Gilsland, about 1¼ miles from Birdoswald (9 min).

As a Roman fort, Birdoswald has nothing new to offer. As a fortified farmhouse that has been in continuous occupation for 2,000 years, it is fascinating. Unfortunately there is no public access to the farmhouse itself, which is now a hostel, but the visitor centre and illustrated interpretive boards by the Roman remains provide the story. Much of it revolves around the Border Reivers: roving bands of Scots and English fighting over land claims.

GOOD EATING
The tea room at Birdoswald sells hot chocolate with whipped cream *and* a flake!

Return to Hexham and continue to Alston or proceed directly to Carlisle.

GETTING to HEXHAM
Bus 185 d. Gilsland for Haltwhistle twice in p.m. (16 min)
Train d. Haltwhistle for Hexham Mo-Su 1/hr (20 min)
Walk to Hexham Bus Station.

GETTING to ALSTON
Bus 888 d. Hexham bus stn for Alston Mo-Sa in the early evening. No Su service except Jul-Sep 1/day in a.m. (50 min)
Motion Sickness Alert!

Alston

There are hairpin bends as well as gentler curves and all too numerous dips. The route, which at first runs through woods and beside rivers, climbs into the Pennines, an area far more barren than around Housesteads.

GETTING to CARLISLE
Bus AD122 d. Birdoswald for Carlisle English St. (45 min)
Bus 185 d. Gilsland for Carlisle, The Courts (45 min)
The bus stops on English Street and The Courts are close to the rail station.

Day 7 – Carlisle

The tour ends at Carlisle. From the railway station you can go north to Scotland, south to London and just about anywhere else, but before heading out try to visit the Tullie House Museum, the castle and the cathedral. They are all close together and not far from the railway station. The City Gate (see map below) is highly visible from the rail station.

Tullie House Museum & Art Gallery
Open Mo-Sa 10.00-17.00
Su (Apr-Jun, Sep-Oct) 12.00-17.00
Su (Jul-Aug) 11.00-17.00
Cost: A £5.20/Co £3.60/Ch £2.60
Tel. 01228 534 781
W: www.tulliehouse.co.uk

Located between the Cathedral and the Castle, Tullie House Museum contains interesting arrangements depicting the history

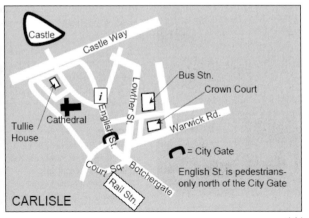

141

of the Borders. There is an excellent Roman section and an audio-visual presentation on the Border Reivers.

A reiver is a thief, but it was more complicated than that. It seems a band of Scots stole a herd of English sheep that were suffering from scab, an infectious disease that passed on to the Scottish sheep. The Scots, incensed at the English for having scabrous sheep apparently begging to be stolen, returned and slaughtered the rightful owners. Thus began four centuries of vengeful theft and pillage.

The truth of that particular story is debatable, but it is probably not far off! Of course, land claims had something to do with it and the fact that the sovereignty of the whole area was under dispute anyway didn't help much.

In the adjacent Old Tullie House are the Gallery of Childhood and displays of Fine and Decorative Arts.

Part of the museum is the medieval Guildhall located opposite the Cathedral.

Carlisle Castle (EH)

Open daily Apr-Sep 9.30-18.00
Oct 10.00-16.00
Cost: A £4.00/Co £3.00/Ch £2.00
Tel. 01228 591 922

The castle was first built in 1092 by William Rufus, the successor to William the Conqueror, as one of the wooden motte and bailey forts thrown up by the Normans to control the north.

It was rebuilt in stone and gradually expanded. Considering it has been fought over by English and Scots, Royalists and Parliamentarians, Jacobites and Hanoverians, it is in remarkably good repair.

The keep contains an exhibition on the Jacobite uprising and on Prince Charles Stuart. Known by romantics as "Bonnie Prince Charlie", the over-ambitious, incompetent soldier and poor organiser died in France: a fat drunkard with plump pink cheeks and a powdered wig. Rather spoils the legend of the romantic and daring "lad born to be king", doesn't it?

Carlisle Cathedral

St. Cuthbert visited Carlisle in 685. His body rested here for part of his 100 years of posthumous travel. For more on Cuthbert see page 20.

Around 1122 a group of Augustinian canons arrived to establish a priory. Eleven years later the diocese of Carlisle was created and the priory church became Carlisle Cathedral.

Parts of the Norman church still stand, identifiable by the rounded shape of some of the arches, including those deformed by subsidence. Examples of Early English and Decorated styles also exist, revealing the structural history of the church. For more on cathedrals, see pages 46 and 47.

At the time of its dissolution by Henry VIII (see page 57), the priory possessed a bit of wood supposedly from the "true cross", Thomas Becket's sword and St. Bridget's girdle. Most its possessions went to the new chapter of the cathedral.

The cathedral was damaged during the Parliamentarian siege of the castle but has been repaired, modified and in continuous use since then.

Getting Home

From Carlisle railway station you can continue to the Lake District (Tour 5) the Cumbrian Coast (Tour 6) and the Eden Valley (Tour 3). Indeed, from Carlisle you can travel easily to just about anywhere in England and Scotland.

Highlights of Tour 5

- Mainline Rail Station: Oxenholme
  - **Ambleside:** [Lake] Windermere for steam railway and aquarium, Grasmere, Blackwell House, Levens Hall and Garden
  - **Hawkshead:** Beatrix Potter Gallery and Hill Top Farm; Coniston Water for lake cruise, Brantwood House and Gardens
  - **Keswick:** Derwentwater, Castlerigg Stone Circle, Honister Pass, Buttermere, Helvellyn without Striding Edge
  - **Glenridding:** Ullswater, lake cruise, Helvellyn via Striding Edge
- Mainline Rail Station: Penrith

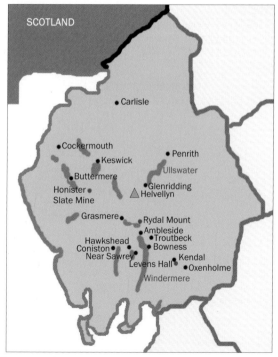

Tour 5 – The Lake District

For most people Cumbria *is* the Lake District. Not surprising, really: there is something about the meres and waters; umber, ochre, grey and green hills; sheep-dotted fields and drystone walls that makes you want to wax poetic or paint or sing or *something*. It's had that effect on people for at least two centuries.

The Lake District covers an area roughly 30 miles by 30 miles in the county of Cumbria. With 42,000 residents and 12 million visitors annually, tourism may be the primary industry, but farming is the core of life here. The farmed landscape is much of what makes the area so beautiful, and it is vital that visitors remember and respect this.

This itinerary uses Ambleside, Hawkshead and Keswick as bases for day trips to suit a variety of tastes, be they walking, literary, artistic or simply enjoyment of the history and scenery as it emerges.

For walkers, many excellent leaflets, maps and books are available at the TICs, book shops and hiking shops. The staff will advise you on where to go depending on your fitness and expertise. The walks described in this tour are simply attractive ways to get from place to place without being too ambitious.

Whatever your walking plans, never underestimate the terrain or the weather! The fells are not particularly high, but they are stony, steep and exposed. The weather is highly changeable, so you might start in high spirits and sunshine in the morning but be mist-bound, chilled and lost with a sprained ankle or broken wrist by mid-afternoon. Please review the Tips for Safe Hiking on page 183.

Handy things to know

It costs up to £100 to repair one yard of footpath. It's really quite an honour to walk on something as expensive as that!

It rains in the Lake District – not all day and not every day, but often. Accept this, don't let it spoil your holiday and *always* take a waterproof jacket and trousers.

Remember, there is no such thing as bad weather — just bad clothes!

Accommodation (see page 10 for abbreviations)

AMBLESIDE, Cumbria
YHA, Waterhead, Ambleside LA22 0EU
Tel. 0870 770 5672; Int (+44) 15394 32304
E: ambleside@yha.org.uk
Cost: £18.50/£14.50 B&B
Open every day; Rec. 7.15-midnight; Laundry

Lattendales, Compston Road, Ambleside LA22 9DJ
Tel. 015394 32368
E: info@lattendales.co.uk   W: www.lattendales.co.uk
Rooms (£pppn): 2Ss (£25-£27); 4De (£27-£32)
No children under 10

Park House Guest House, Compston Road, Ambleside LA22 9DJ
Tel. 015394 31107
E: mail@loughrigg.plus.com   W: www.parkhouseguesthouse.co.uk
Rooms (£pppn): 2Ss, 4De (£25-£36)

Claremont House, Compston Road, Ambleside LA22 9DJ
Tel. 015394 33448; E: enquiries@claremontambleside.co.uk
W: www.claremontambleside.co.uk
Rooms (£pppn): 4De, 2Fe (£25-£32)

HAWKSHEAD, Cumbria
YHA, Hawkshead, Ambleside LA22 0QD
Tel 0870 770 5856; Int (+44) 15394 36293
E: hawkshead@yha.org.uk
Cost £12.50/£9.00
About 20 min walk from Hawkshead TIC. Laundry
Open daily; Rec. 7.15-10.00, 13.00-23.30

Ann Tyson's House, Wordsworth St, Hawkshead, Ambleside LA22 0PA
Tel. 015394 36405; W: www.anntysons.co.uk
Wordsworth lived here.
Rooms (£pppn): 1Se, 5De (£29); 1Dpb (£27.50)

Old School House, Main St, Hawkshead, Ambleside LA22 0NT
Tel. 015394 36403
Rooms (£pppn) 1Tpb, 1Dpb (£24); 3De (£28)

Failing any of these, contact the Hawkshead TIC for more suggestions. Tel. 015394 36525 or E: HawksheadTIC@lake-district.gov.uk

KESWICK, Cumbria
YHA, Station Road, Keswick CA12 5LH
Tel. 0870 770 5894; Int (+44) 17687 72484
Email: keswick@yha.org.uk
Cost: £12.50/£9.00
Open daily; Rec. 7.30-23.00; Laundry

Dalkeith Guest House, 1 Leonard Street, Keswick CA12 4EJ
Tel. 017687 72696
E: info@dalkeithguesthouse.co.uk W: www.dalkeithguesthouse.co.uk
Rooms (£pppn): 1Ss, 1Ds, 1Fs (£22); 1Se, 1Te, 2De (£25)

Glendale Guest House,7 Eskin Street, Keswick CA12 4DH
Tel. 017687 73562
E: info@glendalekeswick.co.uk   W: www.glendalekeswick.co.uk
Rooms (£pppn): 1Ss (£25-£26); 1Ts/Fs (£24-£25), 4De(£25-£26)

HELVELLYN, Cumbria
YHA, Greenside, Glenridding, Penrith CA11 0QR
Located 900 feet up Helvellyn, 1½ miles' walk from the village.
Tel. UK 0870 770 5862; Int (+44) 17684 82269
E: helvellyn@yha.org.uk
Price £11.00/£8.00
Open flexible, Jul/Aug daily; Rec. 8.00-10.00, 17.00-22.00
Meals are excellent!
From Glenridding Pier, follow signs to the village and TIC. When you turn left and see the TIC about 300 yards ahead you will also see a road parallel to the main road and separated from it by a green. Turn right on that road, then left onto a street of dark slate houses. Up the hill are some stone steps, a bench and a wooden sign pointing to the right for Greenside Road. Go to Greenside Road, turn left and follow it to the Youth Hostel. The total walk is about 1½ miles, most of it gently but steadily uphill.

Beech House, Glenridding, Penrith CA11 0TA
Tel. 017684 82037
E: reed@beechhouse.com   W: www.beechhouse.com
Rooms (£pppn): 2Ss (£23-£25); 1Ts, 1Ds (£25); 1Te, 3De (£30)

No. 5 Stybarrow Terrace, Glenridding, Penrith CA11 0QD
Tel. 017684 82248; E: enquiries@stybarrow.co.uk
Rooms (£pppn): 1Ss/Ds, 1Ds (£22)

Base: Ambleside

The railway terminates at the town of Windermere, a mile from the lake of the same name. Adjacent to the lake is Bowness. This bustling holiday resort has a lot to offer but is a bit low on Lakeland character.

Which is why mossy-grey, hill-surrounded Ambleside, a mile north of Waterhead at the top of Windermere, is my preferred base for this area. Just a few minutes'

walk from the fells, it offers accommodation and cafés galore.

A frequent bus service runs from Windermere railway station to Ambleside town centre. Or, take the shuttle bus to Bowness pier, the lake steamer to Waterhead and the electric bus, Thai Tuk Tuk, horse-drawn carriage or just walk to Ambleside town centre.

At Waterhead you can rent a

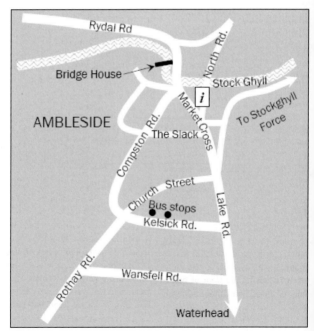

boat, feed the ducks, avoid the swans, go for a swim, eat ice cream or visit a tea room. The youth hostel is here.

All Ambleside buses stop at Kelsick Road (see map).

GETTING to AMBLESIDE
Mainline rail station: OXENHOLME
Train d. Oxenholme for Windermere Mo-Sa about 1/hr, Su every 1-2 hr (20 min)

Buses 505, 518, 555, 599, 618 d. Windermere rail stn for Waterhead and Ambleside Mo-Su 3-4/hr (15 min)

Ambleside is a largely Victorian town surrounded by Loughrigg Fell, Wansfell and Fairfield Fell – all good for moderately energetic walks.

An easy stroll for your first day is to Stockghyll Force, a woodland waterfall one mile east of the centre of Ambleside. Follow the lane heading out of the town on the right of the Salutation hotel.

St. Mary the Virgin Church

This 19[th]C church built by Sir Gilbert Scott is distinguished by its tall steeple and the contemporary mural of a Rush-Bearing Ceremony. It was a medieval custom to strew rushes on the floor of buildings to absorb moisture and mask smells. The procedure has become a tradition with a parade of children carrying rushes to the church on the first Saturday in July.

William Wordsworth contributed to the construction of the church, which has commemorative windows for himself, his wife Mary, sister Dorothy and daughter Dora.

Bridge House National Trust Shop and Information centre

Open daily 10.00-17.00
Tel. 015394 32617
E: windermere
@nationaltrust.org.uk

Bridge House was built in 1723 as a combination apple store and bridge. It is now a National Trust shop; these are always worth visiting. For all its fame, it can be surprisingly difficult to find: it melts so into its surroundings. See map for its location.

Armitt Ambleside Museum

Open daily 10.00-17.00
Cost: A £2.50/CoCh £1.80
Tel. 015394 31212
W: www.armitt.com

Most people know Beatrix Potter as the creator of Peter Rabbit; few may be aware of her contributions to natural history. The Armitt Museum holds over 400 of her studies of fungi and mosses, as well as her detailed drawings of Roman artefacts from Galava – the only existing record of some items that have long since disintegrated.

149

Ambleside Roman Fort (NT/EH)
Unrestricted access; Cost: free
Tel. 015394 46027
E: windermere
@nationaltrust.org.uk

On the right hand side of the road as you approach Waterhead is a field with a couple of small enclosures and, possibly, a herd of cattle. The enclosures protect raised turf outlines: all that remain of Galava, a Roman fort built around AD74 to protect the area from invading Picts and Scots. Items from the fort are on display at the Armitt Ambleside Museum.

BASE: AMBLESIDE
Day Trip – The Wordsworth Walk (or bus tour)

Whether you are a Wordsworth fan or not, this day out is a delight.

Grasmere and Rydal Water are two little lakes joined by the River Rothay. Grasmere is idyllic: not quite a mile long and possessing its own island, it is protected from the barren fells by soft green slopes and fairy-tale woods carpeted with daffodils in April and bluebells in May. See it once in sunshine and it will remain forever thus in your memory.

Grasmere village is a gem. It has a pub, bistro and bookshop: can you ask for anything more? The Gingerbread Shop is in the original 1630 village school where Wordsworth occasionally taught. Next door is St. Oswald's church.

Rydal Water has a busy road along one side and a bald fell on the other. In spite of these disadvantages the fell-side approach provides an attractive view and the return route follows the road for just a short distance.

The entire circular walk is about five miles along mostly level paths with a couple of short hilly bits and some road walking.

If you can't manage the entire route, the frequency of buses allows any combination of walking and bussing to suit individual requirements.

A Bit of History
William Wordsworth was born in Cockermouth on 7 April 1770. One of many poets and writers to find peace and inspiration in the Lake District, he rented the *Dove and Olive Bough*, a cramped and aged inn close to the shore of Grasmere.

He moved in with his sister Dorothy in 1799. By 1808 Dove Cottage, as it was now called, housed William, his wife Mary and their three children, as well as

Mary's sister Sara and Dorothy. With another child in the making larger quarters were called for. The Wordsworths moved a few times before settling into Rydal Mount, near Rydal Water, in 1813. Here they lived until William's death in 1850.

Rydal Mount is still owned by descendants of Wordsworth, but is maintained by the Wordsworth Trust, as are Dove Cottage and its adjacent museum.

GETTING to GRASMERE

Bus 599 open-top double-decker bus d. Ambleside for Grasmere Mo-Su 3/hr (2/hr Sep, Oct) (6 min to Rydal Church for Rydal Mount, 20 min to Grasmere village for Dove Cottage)

Buses 555 and 556 d. Ambleside for Grasmere 1/hr Mo-Su (6 min to Rydal Church, 16 min to Grasmere village)

Plan to lunch at Grasmere, or assemble a picnic in Ambleside for eating en route from Rydal Mount to Dove Cottage.

The walk starts at Rydal Mount while you have the energy to explore the terraced gardens, then proceeds to Grasmere and a visit to St. Oswald's church, where the Wordsworths are buried. Next is Dove Cottage and the Wordsworth Museum. Complete the circuit by returning to Rydal Church.

THE WALK

Ask the bus driver to drop you off at Rydal Church. To the right of the church is an uphill lane that leads to Rydal Mount, which is on the left side of the lane and is not to be confused with Rydal Hall, which is on the right.

After visiting the house and gardens return down the lane to the main road [Bus Stop for Grasmere] and turn right. Cross the road and continue, first on the pavement, then on the footpath, until you see a car park on your left. Turn in and straight ahead is a map on a board. Keep to the left of the board and follow the path marked as wheelchair accessible over a short wooden footbridge and towards the river.

Do not cross the footbridge that soon comes up on the left. Instead, go through the gate ahead of you and continue along the well-defined gravel path, within hearing of the river. When the path drops back down to the river, cross the long footbridge and turn right. You are now within sight of Grasmere (the lake).

Cross the pebbled beach and pass through a gate to another well-defined path with the lake on your right. This path follows the lakeshore then turns sharply left, uphill, and terminates on a narrow road bordered by moss-

151

covered walls on both sides. Turn right and follow the road, keeping an eye and ear out for traffic, to Grasmere. St. Oswald's church is on the left.

Go through the gate into the churchyard, where you can see the Wordsworths' gravestones, then visit the interior of the church.

Exit the church yard via the arch with the Gingerbread Shop on the right. Take some time to rest, eat and explore the village. [Bus Stop for Dove Cottage and Ambleside]

Return through the arch to the churchyard and exit through the gate whence you originally came. Turn left, go over the hump-backed bridge and continue along the road. When it curves to the right you will see Grasmere lake again on your right, and, shortly after that, there is a mini-roundabout. Keep following the road to the right. Follow the signs to the Wordsworth Trust. You will

see a grey slate cylindrical building beside a larger building with a curved end wall. This is the Wordsworth Museum. Go to the museum for tickets to Dove Cottage.

When you have finished visiting the cottage and museum, return to the road [Bus Stop for Ambleside], turn left and continue beside the lake until the road zigzags and a footpath into some woods opens up in front of you.

There are several paths and a small yellow arrow on a post. Take the main path that angles to the right, more or less in the direction the arrow points. When the path splits take the left option along the gravelled path and over a little footbridge. The path will take you down to the river and the long footbridge that you crossed on the way to Grasmere.

Cross the long footbridge again and keep following the main path to the left until you arrive at another footbridge. Don't cross this bridge, but stand with it at your back: the path to your right is the one you just came along. Moving anti-clockwise you will see another path heading uphill. Follow that path a few minutes, then go through the kissing gate (see page 97 if you don't know what a kissing gate is) and take the path downhill to the left (unless you

Bluebell woods by Grasmere

want to follow Loughrigg Terrace, in which case you proceed straight ahead). The downhill path takes you close to the lake (Rydal Water) with a drystone wall on your left. When you get to the far end of the lake, go through the metal kissing gate and continue along the path until you reach the main road. Turn right and in about 100 yards, on the far side of the road, is the bus stop near Rydal Church.

The entire route, including Dove Cottage, the Wordsworth Museum and Rydal Mount, but not including lunch, takes about 5 – 5½ hr.

Rydal Mount
Open daily 9.30-17.00
Cost: A £4.50/Co £3.50-£3.75/ Ch £1.50/Garden only £2.00

Discount with bus ticket or YHA card. Discount brochure for Dove Cottage and Rydal Mount
Tel. 015394 33002
W: www.rydalmount.co.uk

Rydal Mount was the home of William Wordsworth from 1813 until his death in 1850. The greater part of the house was built in 1750 around a 16thC cottage, which is now the dining room. Apart from the dining room, it all looks a little too contemporary and chilly for my taste; however, there are family portraits and some of Wordsworth's belongings, as well as access to the bedrooms and his study.

The four-acre garden is beautiful and the views are fantastic! There are terraces, wooded bits

Dove Cottage and Wordsworth Museum

and waterfalls, while adjacent is Dora's Field – a steep, wooded slope carpeted with daffodils in April and bluebells in May. Beside the field is St. Mary's church, designed by Wordsworth.

If you are on a tight budget I suggest getting the garden-only ticket and save your funds for Dove Cottage and the Museum.

Dove Cottage and Wordsworth Museum

Open daily 9.30-17.00
Cost: A £6.00/Ch £3.75
Discount with bus ticket or YHA card. Discount brochure for Dove Cottage and Rydal Mount
Tel. 015394 35544
W: www.wordsworth.org.uk

Dove Cottage is small, cramped and cosy. It must have been very cosy with Wordsworth's wife, three children, sister and sister-in-law, together with sundry lovers and poets all packed in. Himself would occasionally climb out of a window to escape!

An enthusiastic and knowledgeable guide will take you around the cottage, entertaining you with facts, gossip and scandal. All but the front room are furnished with the Wordsworths' belongings.

The garden may not be open, depending on the condition of the ground.

The adjacent museum is a recent and, from an architectural point of view, moderately controversial addition. In fact it blends comfortably with its surroundings and looks just fine. It contains a wide selection of sketches and paintings (including a Gainsborough) as well as a vast quantity of Wordsworth and friends memorabilia.

St. Oswald's Church

In 1811 the Wordsworth family moved into the rectory, which was not in church use at the time. Two of the children died there.

At that time the church had a rush-strewn dirt floor with burials in the aisle. The rush-bearing ceremony is still held on the Saturday nearest to 5 August (St. Oswald's day).The slate flagstones were installed in 1840.

The church was responsible for education, hence the village school in the little Gingerbread Shop by the churchyard gate. Wordsworth, Mary, Dorothy and Sara all taught there.

After moving to Rydal Mount the Wordsworths continued to attend St. Oswald's Church. There is a memorial in the church and their grave is in the yard.

St Oswald was a Northumbrian king whose story is related on

page 19. His head is usually shown held by St. Cuthbert. Another part of his body that seems to lead a separate post mortem existence is his hand. On the north west corner of the church sanctuary is a processional cross depicting the hand of the saint, and a carved stone shaft thought to be from a 12thC cross.

St. Oswald's Church is, in the words of Wordsworth, "large and massy…with pillars crowded, and the roof upheld by naked rafters intricately crossed…"

The tower walls are about four feet thick, made of boulders and mortar, now under a layer of concrete to keep out the weather.

The tower and the nave are the oldest parts of the church. The aisle to the north (on the left when facing the altar) is a later addition built to accommodate a larger congregation. The original north wall was retained, but arches were cut into it and a second roof was built over the new aisle. Later, a single roof covered both nave and aisle and a second row of arches was added to the wall to support the higher roof.

BASE: AMBLESIDE

Day Trip – Farms and Fells

The Lake District National Park Visitor Centre at Brockhole is a short bus ride from Ambleside. Here you will find an interesting and thoughtful display of the Lake District, the people who live there and the people who visit.

From here a two-mile walk leads to the upland village of Troutbeck to visit the house of a yeoman farmer.

Then you hit the fells in earnest, with a moderately strenuous two-hour walk over Wansfell Pike (1,588 feet) back to Ambleside. This makes a good introduction to fell walking. Please read the Tips for Safe Hiking on page 183.

Alternatively, retrace your path to the main road for a bus to Ambleside or on to Bowness.

> GETTING to BROCKHOLE
> Bus 599 d. Ambleside for Brockhole Mo-Su 3/hr (2/hr Sep, Oct)
> Buses 555 and 556 d.Ambleside Mo-Su 1/hr. Ask for Brockhole (8 min).
> OR
> Brockhole Launch Service, d. Waterhead 1/hr (2/hr Aug-Sep)

The Lake District National Park Visitor Centre, Brockhole
Open daily 10.00-17.00
Cost: free
Tel. 015394 46601
W: www.lake-district.gov.uk

The National Park *is* the Lake District. The exhibition, which just avoids preachiness, uses videos, audio tapes, dioramas and traditional displays to enhance your appreciation of this unique and precious area that is in perpetual danger of being trampled to death.

There is an interesting history of local tourism that relates visitors' opinions, which ranged from unfavourable (a barren, wind- and rain-swept wilderness) to inspirational (poets and painters).

The exhibition, gift shop, café, adventure playground and games lawn are located within extensive gardens that run down to the lake.

The café provides sandwiches, a limited selection of hot meals, traditional cakes and, on peak days, a salad bar.

GETTING to TOWNEND by FOOT
Note: There is an infrequent bus service – see the end this tour.
From Brockhole turn left on the main road and walk about ten minutes until you reach Holbeck Lane on the right. It is signposted Townend 1½ miles, Troutbeck 2½ miles.

From the signpost it takes about 40 min to walk to Townend. Although mostly uphill, there are enough level bits and splendid views for the walk not to be as painful or tiring as it might sound. The road is narrow, with no verges, so keep alert for traffic.

A sign for Townend parking lot will appear on your left.

Townend House (NT)

Open We-Su/BH 13.00-17.00
Cost: A £3.40/Ch £1.70
Tel. 015394 32628
E: townend@nationaltrust.org.uk

The house was owned by the Browne family from 1626 to 1943 and retains the features that characterise the home of a yeoman farmer – one who owned the land he farmed.

There are bedrooms for two

Drystone wall between Troutbeck and Wansfell

maids and a housekeeper, and a very long table in the Fire House (the main heated room on the ground floor) where the family, servants and farmhands all ate.

The Browne men had a passion for wood carving on a grand scale: on fireplaces, chairs, cupboards, beds and chests. Look for the Maori-influenced work and 24 or so faces carved into the woodwork of the main bedroom.

The Brownes owned a large eclectic collection of books. While you can only peer through the library door, texts from some of the books are copied and placed in the hall for your perusal.

The pretty garden is based on a description from about 1900 – a riot of cottage garden flowers enclosed, not very successfully, by formal patterns of low hedges.

To reach Troutbeck exit Townend, turn left and continue along the road for about five minutes. The village is best known for its pub, "The Mortal Man", now an upscale inn.

If a fell walk is not for you, retrace your steps and pick up the 555 or 599 bus back to Ambleside or on to Bowness.

If you do plan to do the fell walk, check the sky before heading out over Wansfell. Although the path is fairly well defined, it is rough in places and you should avoid being on the fells in a cloud.

THE WALK: TROUTBECK to AMBLESIDE

For Wansfell, exit Townend, turn left and continue along the road until you reach Troutbeck Post Office on your left (5-6 min). Immediately before the Post Office, Robin's Lane meets the road at a shallow angle.

Follow the lane, which starts gently uphill between stone walls, then flattens out along more open ground among the fells. The lane seems to go on forever, but keep following it straight ahead until it ends beside a stream and little waterfalls. It gets a bit trickier from here because the path is very faint.

Go through the gate and follow the sign for Wansfell to the right. You will be standing on sheep-shorn grass and the path is not immediately obvious. Look for a small white arrow on a post and follow that while looking out for the next one.

You will climb over a wall, using the steps built into it, and continue following the white arrows which will lead you uphill, roughly parallel to the stone wall. When you come to a kissing gate in the wall with a little yellow arrow pointing to the left and another to the right, go through the kissing gate and the serious walking begins.

The path is clearly defined, but take it steadily and carefully, as the footing is uneven. You will probably start to appreciate the labour that goes into creating and maintaining these tracks.

Whenever you pause to get your breath remember to look at the view! When you reach the summit, you will agree the hike is worth the effort (unless you are in a cloud).

The path descends steeply down man-made steps and terminates on a road that leads back to Ambleside, passing Stockghyll Force and the Salutation Hotel.

ALTERNATIVE ROUTE to TROUTBECK

It is possible to get close to Troutbeck by bus; however, the bus drops you at the Queen's Head, from where it is a short, but steep walk to the village proper and Townend.

From Ambleside, take bus 555 or 599 to Windermere rail stn.

Bus 517 d. Windermere rail stn for Troutbeck 3/day. Mid-Jul to end Aug Mo-Su; Apr-mid-Jul & Sep, Oct on Sa, Su/BH (12 min).

BASE: AMBLESIDE

Day Trip – Windermere, the Lake

The shores of Windermere provide activities and sights to cover most tastes. From Waterhead, cruise to Bowness where, tucked between the ice cream and souvenir shops at the piers and the steamboat museum less than ten minutes walk to the north, lies a pretty Lakeland village complete with the Hole in t'Wall pub.

The Bowness TIC has a wide range of maps and is located just to the right of the piers as you disembark from the steamers.

A 30-minute walk south is Blackwell House. It has an Arts & Crafts Movement interior and gardens extending to the lake.

From Bowness, cruise to Lakeside at the southern tip of Windermere for a steam-train ride, the Aquarium of the Lakes and a Victorian country park.

You won't have time to see it all, so take your pick and remember it is always colder and windier on a lake than on shore.

GETTING to WINDERMERE (THE LAKE) & BOWNESS

Walk, take the horse-drawn carriage, electric bus, Tuk Tuk or bus to Waterhead. Look for the Windermere Lake Cruises ticket office (hard to miss).

The cruise schedule varies. Roughly, boats leave Waterhead for Bowness twice hourly and from Bowness to Lakehead hourly. The Haverthwaite train connects with the boat at Lakehead. Schedules are available in guest houses, TIC and the cruise ticket office.

You can get just about any combination of tickets with a variety of savings, so just tell the ticket office your plans for the day. Some fares:

Freedom of the Lake
A £12.50/Ch £6.25
Combined Boat and Train
A £15.60/Ch £8.25
Combined Boat and Aquarium
A £17.80/Ch £9.60

Blackwell House
Open daily 10.30-17.00
Cost: A £5.00/CoCh £2.75
Tel. 015394 46139
W: www.blackwell.org.uk

GETTING to BLACKWELL HOUSE
From Bowness Pier by BUS:
May-Sep Mo-Su; Apr & Oct Sa, Su/BH & school holidays the Windermere-Bowness Shuttle Bus Service detours to Blackwell Arts & Craft House *once* an hour (7 min)

ON FOOT: From Bowness Pier turn right (south) and follow the A592 (The Promenade) south. When the road diverges take the left branch up the hill towards Kendal and Lancaster. From this point the RAC has posted white-on-blue signs to Blackwell Arts & Craft House. At the next major intersection turn right (A5074 to Lancaster and Lyth Valley).

After some nice views of the lake, there will be another sign pointing to the right (B5360). About level with this sign there is a dip in the wall to your right. Have a look over for a hedge maze in the garden. Later there is a black on white sign for Blackwell pointing to the right, then right again into the drive.

The walk is largely uphill, but not overly strenuous, and there are quite a few level bits. On some stretches there is no pavement, so keep an ear out for approaching traffic. Distance is about 1½ miles, walking time about 35 minutes.

Blackwell House was built between 1898 and 1900 as a holiday home for the Manchester brewer Sir Edward Holt. It is the only house designed by Arts & Craft proponent Mackay Hugh Baillie Scott that is open to the public.

William Morris, the leader of the Arts & Crafts Movement, believed that the mass production of cheap goods contributed to the social problems of the time. He felt that art and production should complement each other, that artist-craftsmen should produce high quality consumer goods that are both functional and beautiful.

Characteristic of the Arts & Crafts Movement, which predates and influenced Art Nouveau, are stained glass windows, hand-painted tiles, hand-woven rugs and the inspiration of flowers and plants in the design. All these are evident at Blackwell House.

The interior is based on a medieval theme applied in contemporary terms. The result is very successful: spacious, light and elegant, yet comfortable and welcoming. The house is a delight for anyone even remotely interested in interior design and decorating (and how many people aren't?)

Windermere was incorporated into the landscape design. The formality of the gardens near the house diminishes towards the lake.

The cost of admission includes a good descriptive leaflet. Post cards of the interior are available in the gift shop, which also has a good selection of art and design books. Allow at least 45 minutes to view the house: longer to explore the grounds.

There is a small café, very busy at lunch time.

Windermere Steamboats & Museum

Open daily 10.00-17.00
Cost: A £4.75/Co £4.25/Ch £2.50
Cruise: A £5.50/Ch £2.25
Discount for two or more YHA
Tel. 015394 45565
W: www.steamboat.co.uk

GETTING to the WINDERMERE STEAMBOATS & MUSEUM
From Bowness Pier turn left (north) on the main road and keep to the left when it diverges. It will become Rayrigg Road and the museum is on the left (10 min)

There are steamboats, motor boats from 1898 to the present and a Hydroplane Racing boat. From the

Hole in t'Wall, Bowness on Windermere

ilm version of Arthur Ransome's children's novel *Swallows and Amazons* is the sailboat *Amazon* and Captain Flint's houseboat, which you can explore if a guide is available. There are model boat demonstrations near the picnic area on Thursday and Sunday.

Check ahead for the availability of the fifty-minute cruise around Belle Isle on a classic steam-launch. The cruise includes tea or coffee and biscuits and usually runs five times a day subject to the weather, maintenance and staff availability.

Allow about 30 to 45 minutes for your visit. There is also a good gift shop and a café.

GETTING to LAKESIDE
Take the Yellow Cruise from Bow-ness to Lakeside (40 min)

Lakeside and Haverthwaite Railway

The train platform is behind the café beside the pier. Trains connect with the boat and run daily from 23 Apr. The round trip lasts ¾ hour and includes a stop of about ten to fifteen minutes at Haverthwaite.

Cost (return) A £4.70/Ch £2.35
Tel. 015395 31594
W: www.lakesiderailway.co.uk

For steam railway enthusiasts this is another for the collection. For everyone else it is a moderately scenic train ride beside the River Leven, mostly through woods.

Children particularly enjoy it.

Aquarium of the Lakes

Open daily 9.00-18.00, last admission 17.00

Herdwick Sheep. The name Herdwick (pr. exactly as spelled, oddly enough) derives from "Herdwycks", meaning sheep pastures.

Cost: A £6.25/Co £5.50/Ch £3.95
Tel. 015395 30153
W: www.aquariumofthelakes.co.uk

The aquarium is on the far side of the train platform. It may look closed, because the entrance is dark even when it is open.

The aquarium is worth a visit if only for the otters, harvest mice and water voles! The fish displays are well laid out and the whole is fun and interesting. Allow at least 45 minutes.

Fell Foot Park (NT)

Open daily 9.00-17.00
Shop and tea room 11.00-17.00
Cost: free
Tel. 015395 31273
E: fellfootpark@nationaltrust.org.uk

There are three ferries an hour from Lakeside to Fell Foot Park from 10.00-16.20. This Victorian country park offers rowing boats for hire, family activities, gardens, a licensed tea room and packed lunches (provided by Trusty the Hedgehog). Contact the property for updates on special events.

BASE: AMBLESIDE
Day Trip – Kendal

A visit to the Elizabethan manor and topiary gardens of Levens Hall is something not to miss. En route the bus stops at the market town of Kendal, which is worth a visit in its own right.

Kendal is the birthplace of Catherine Parr, the sixth wife of Henry VIII. Located on the edge of the Lake District, it is less popular than nearby Ambleside and Bowness, yet is full of grey limestone buildings, intriguing little alleys that lead to yards bounded by houses, shops and restaurants. The River Kent runs through and there is a ruined castle on a hill. An alley of trees around the park creates a mini-arboretum.

Make sure you try some Kendal Mint Cake, available at most sweetie shops in the Lake District and hardly anywhere else. As a compact energy source it is hard to beat, as attested by Sir Edmund Hillary, who took a supply on his successful Everest expedition with Tenzing Norgay in 1953.

Levens Hall is closed on Friday and Saturday; the Museum of Lakeland Life and Abbot Hall are closed on Sunday. Visiting Levens Hall should be your priority.

If you arrive at Levens Hall no later than 11.00 you will have an hour to stroll through the gardens before the house opens. After visiting the house and lunching at the

Bellingham Buttery, return to Kendal to explore the town.

GETTING to LEVENS HALL from AMBLESIDE

Bus 555 d. Kelsick Road for Levens Bridge, directly across the road from Levens Hall Mo-Sa 1/hr (68 min)

On Su: Bus 555 d. Kelsick Road for Kendal bus stn 1/hr (39 min)
Bus X55 d. Kendal bus stn every 2 hr for Levens Hall (10 min)

Levens Hall

Open mid-Apr to mid-Oct, Su-Th
Gardens, Buttery Tea Room, Gift Shop 10.00-17.00
House 12.00-17.00
Cost
House & Gardens: A £9.00/Ch £4.00
Gardens only: A £6.00/Ch £3.00
Discount for YHA £1.00
Tel. 015395 60321
W: www.levenshall.co.uk

Levens Hall started as a late 13thC pele tower or fortification. It was expanded in the late sixteenth century and again 100 years later. The medieval tower remains at the heart of the house.

It is said that Levens was won through gambling at cards – by the turn of an ace of hearts. Just before entering the house look at the downspout to the right of the door to see the single heart insignia.

The various owners of the house resisted change, so the original dark panelling and decorative plastered ceilings typical of the Elizabethan era remain. The effect makes Levens Hall different from most stately homes, which have been updated over the centuries to match changes in fashion.

Of particular interest is the leather panelling to be found in the Dining Room and in the small bedroom that also houses the Duke of Wellington's campaign bed.

Allow at least an hour to explore the late 17thC gardens, which are justly famous for the topiary. Like guests at a genteelly tipsy tree party, the coiffed and corseted trees incline politely to each other while a pair of shocked little birds turn their pertly cocked tails to the disgraceful proceedings.

The topiary is just part of the whole magical area. There are all kinds of secret gardens lurking behind and within staidly regimented hedges.

There is a play area for children with a miniature commando course, *Bertha* the steam engine and *Little Gem*, a smaller engine that takes children for rides around the grounds on Sundays and Bank Holidays.

GOOD EATING

The *Bellingham Buttery Tea Room* provides refreshments and

lunches from 10.00. On offer are salads, sandwiches and traditional cakes, all made from local produce, as well as hot and cold drinks.

Try to avoid Bank Holiday weekends as crowds detract from the pleasure of the place. In particular, the gardens are probably best seen on a slightly damp, misty morning when you might glimpse the ghosts of a little black dog and a gypsy woman.

RETURN to KENDAL
Leave Levens Hall, turn left and follow the pavement *around the corner* to the left. The stop for Bus 555 is clearly indicated.

Kendal bus station is on Blackhall Road. To reach the town centre

Levens Hall topiary garden

walk back to the first intersection and turn right into Stramongate. At the next intersection, either turn right to the market place or continue straight ahead on Finkle Street; both end on Stricklandgate the main pedestrian area. Turn left and just before the road (Lowther Street) you will find the TIC on the left.

From the TIC cross Lowther Street and immediately look out on the left for a very narrow alley that leads to the riverside walk. Turn right for the arboretum, parish church, museum and art gallery.

Museum of Lakeland Life & Industry

Open Mo-Sa 10.30-17.00
Cost: A £3.75/CoCh £2.75
Discounted tickets if you visit Abbot Hall Art Gallery on the same day
Tel. 01539 722 464
W: www.lakelandmuseum.org.uk

This museum is good fun. You start by walking along an early 19thC street, continue through the workshops of various craftsmen and finally visit a private home.

The author of *Swallows and Amazons*, Arthur Ransome, is represented by a mock-up of his study with his drawings and papers on view. If you take the trip to Coniston (see page 169) you will see the locations mentioned in the book.

Abbot Hall Art Gallery

Open Mo-Sa 10.30-17.00
Cost: A £4.75 (£3.75 for permanent collection only). Discounted tickets if you visit the Museum of Lakeland Life & Industry on the same day
Tel. 01539 722 464
W: www.abbothall.org.uk

This small airy art gallery, adapted from a Georgian villa, houses a collection of watercolours by such artists as Turner, Constable, Lear and Ruskin. There are portraits by Romney, a Hockney and an exquisite grouping of miniatures. Contemporary artists are the focus of changing exhibitions.

The Parish Church

The stonework of the nave is early twelfth century. The is a modern sculpture by Josephina de Vasconcellos, whose work appears in many churches in the area.

Base: Ambleside or Hawkshead

The next two day trips can be taken from either Ambleside or Hawkshead, a village in the fells at the north end of Esthwaite Water.

The Beatrix Potter Gallery is in the centre of Hawkshead. Hill Top Farm is a two-mile walk or eight-minute bus journey away.

William Wordsworth and his brother attended the grammar school here, and Anne Tyson's cottage, where they boarded whilst attending the school, is now a Bed & Breakfast – one of the few in Hawkshead. That is the only problem with this lovely place: the small number of places to stay.

If you plan to make Hawkshead your base for these day trips book early and don't forget to visit The World of Beatrix Potter Attraction whilst staying in Ambleside.

GETTING to HAWKSHEAD
Bus 505 d. Ambleside Kelsick Rd for Hawkshead Mo-Sa 1/hr; Su every 1-2 hr (20 min)

Day Trip – The Beatrix Potter Trail

The trail starts at Bowness for The World of Beatrix Potter Attraction, heads across Windermere by ferry then, by foot or by bus, climbs up to Hill Top Farm at Near Sawrey. It continues (by foot or by bus) to Hawkshead for the Beatrix Potter Gallery. From Hawkshead return to Ambleside by bus.

About Beatrix Potter

The sun probably never sets on the readers of Beatrix Potter's little books, yet she would probably have preferred not to be remembered solely as the creator of Peter Rabbit, for she was so much more.

In some ways, her books were simply the means to an end.

Beatrix Potter was an artist, storyteller, scientist, farmer, conservationist and breeder of prize-winning Herdwicks, hardy sheep unique to the Lake District.

Beatrix was born in 1866 to rigidly Victorian middle class parents in London. She was educated at home and seems rarely to have left the nursery or school room, where she read, played with her pets (including her rabbit Peter), drew and painted. From the age of sixteen Beatrix accompanied her family to the Lake District for their summer holidays, but it was not until she was thirty that they went to Sawrey.

When in London she spent much of her time at Kew Gardens. She painted highly detailed scientific illustrations of fungi and was the first person to observe the germination of the spores of a fungus *Agaricineae*. The paper she wrote on the subject when she was sixteen was ignored until 1897, when it was read at the Linnean Society, a scientific group dedicated primarily to taxonomy and classification. Four hundred of her scientific paintings are now at the Armitt Museum in Ambleside.

The sales of *The Tale of Peter Rabbit*, published in 1902, allowed

her to buy Hill Top Farm in 1905. Although close to forty, she was still obliged to live with her parents. She spent most of her time in London but kept a close watch on the farm and, with its manager John Cannon, improved and expanded the flock of Herdwick sheep. In 1909 she bought Castle Farm, which borders Hill Top.

In 1913, very much against her parents' wishes, she married her solicitor, William Heelis. They moved to Castle Farm but Beatrix used Hill Top as her study.

Beatrix enthusiastically supported the work of the National Trust, and, over the next thirty years, she bought property, improved the land and stock and raised money through her drawings. She worked to keep large estates intact, to protect land from developers and to ensure public access to the lakes.

When she died in 1943 she bequeathed over 4,000 acres to the National Trust.

GETTING to the WORLD of BEATRIX POTTER ATTRACTION
Bus 599 d. Ambleside for Bowness Pier Mo-Su 3/hr (2/hr Sep,Oct) (26 min)
OR
Launch d. Waterhead for Bowness Pier every ½ - 1 hr (30 min).
From Bowness Pier follow the

main road (The Promenade) to the left. When it splits, take the right branch (Crag Brow) and look for the attraction on the right.

The World of Beatrix Potter Attraction

Open daily 10.00-17.30
Cost: A £5.00/Ch £4.00
Tel. 015394 88444
W: www.hop-skip-jump.com

Unless your sense of wonder has decayed to hopeless cynicism you will love The World of Beatrix Potter. Indeed, it is hard to imagine anyone not enjoying it! Life-size scenes from all the little books have been created by set designers of the National Theatre and the Royal Shakespeare Company. The scenes are as exquisite as the original paintings and are a delight to see. An introductory film relates the tale of Beatrix Potter.

GOOD EATING

The *Tailor of Gloucester Tea Room* won the 2004 Local Food & Drink Award. You never know whom you will meet as you enjoy lunch or tea!

Proceed to Hill Top Farm

GETTING to HILL TOP FARM

Two services cross Windermere on the first leg of the trip to Hill Top and Hawkshead.
BY BOAT AND FOOT: From Bowness Pier follow the main road (The Promenade) to the right. After passing Glebe Road twice on the right (it's a crescent) look out for Ferry Nab Road. Turn right and proceed to Ferry Nab (not quite ¾ mile from Bowness Pier).
The passenger and car ferry d. Ferry Nab for Ash Landing Mo-Su 10.00-17.00 3/hr (5 min)
Walk from Ash Landing to Hill Top Farm and Near Sawrey along a signposted footpath (2 miles). A map is available from Bowness TIC. The scenery is very pleasant, but part of the route is along a narrow and busy road without a pavement, so look and listen for traffic.

BY BOAT AND BUS: The Cross Lakes Shuttle passenger launch d. Bowness Pier 3 for Ash Landing May-Sep daily, Apr & Oct Sa, Su/BH and school holidays at intervals of about one hour from 10.00 until 16.30 (15 min)
Bus 525 connects with the launch for Hill Top at Near Sawrey (5 min) and Hawkshead (8 min from Hill Top). Pick up a current Cross Lakes Shuttle timetable from Bowness TIC or Tel. 015394 45161.

Whether you arrive by bus or foot, you will need to walk 100 yards beyond the Tower Bank Arms pub to the Ticket Office, which is tucked away at the far left corner of what is easy to mistake for a hotel parking lot. With your ticket, which will have a time on it, return to the road and walk 200 yards back to the entrance of Hill Top. No tickets sold after 16.00

Hill Top (NT)

Open House Sa-We 10.30-16.30 by timed ticket only.
Garden and Shop Sa-We 10.30-17.00; Th, Fr 10.00-17.00
Cost: A £5.00/Ch £2.00
Discount with ticket from Beatrix Potter Gallery.
Access to Garden free on Th & Fr
Tel. 015394 36269
E: hilltop@nationaltrust.org.uk

Walking the narrow garden path to the front door of Hill Top is like walking into one of the Tales. The illusion persists as you creep through the cramped cottage: here is the tailor of Gloucester's dresser and there is Tabitha Twitchit's teapot, while on the stairs you expect to see a dapper rat pushing a rolling pin!

What you won't see is artwork by Beatrix Potter. Instead, there is a collection of Victorian oils and water-colours including works by her brother Bertram. Amazingly, considering his unsmiling face, the whimsical blue animals on the plates in the entrance hall were painted by her father, Rupert Potter.

This fine example of a period farm house is a very popular at-

traction, best visited outside peak tourist season. Even if you can't see inside the house, the garden is definitely worth the trip.

GETTING to the BEATRIX POTTER GALLERY in HAWKSHEAD
Pick up Bus 525 from Near Sawrey (8 min) or continue along the narrow and busy road another two miles to Hawkshead.

Beatrix Potter Gallery (NT)

Open Gallery Sa-We 10.30-16.30
Shop daily 10.30-16.30
Cost: A £3.50/Ch £1.70
Discount with ticket from Hill Top
Tel. 015394 36355
E: beatrixpottergallery@nationaltrust.org.uk

Housed in the late Victorian/early Edwardian law office of Beatrix's husband William Heelis, the wide variety of watercolours, sketches and displays shows the vast extent of her interests and talents.

Like Hill Top farm, the gallery is worth visiting in its own right.

The shop sells Peter Rabbit and friends-related items and a range of Herdwick wool products.

RETURN to AMBLESIDE
Bus 505 d. Hawkshead TIC for Ambleside Mo-Sa 1/hr; Su every 1-2 hr (20 min)
WARNING: Be at the stop at least 10 minutes ahead of time. The bus may leave early.

BASE: AMBLESIDE or HAWKSHEAD

Day Trip – Coniston

As you head from Ambleside up to Coniston, the hills become sharper and starker. Coniston Water is about six miles long and half a mile across, making it the third largest lake in the Lake District.

In his children's story *Swallows and Amazons* Arthur Ransome turns quiet Coniston Water into a tempest-tossed ocean with strange inhabitants on unexplored shores. A band of brave adventurers land on deserted Wildcat Island and sail the dangerous waters where ruthless pirates lurk in the River Amazon.

You can trace this wonderful adventure of the imagination on board one of the solar-powered Coniston Launches, M.L. *Ransome* or M.L. *Ruskin*.

Coniston has a darker side: on 4 January 1967 Donald Campbell attempted a new world water speed record in the jet-powered *Bluebird*. As he reached an estimated 320 mph he hit a patch of turbulence and died in the resulting somersault. His remains and those of *Bluebird* were retrieved in 2001.

John Ruskin, the artist, philosopher and art critic, lived at Brantwood on the east shore from 1872 until his death in 1900.

The village of Coniston, on the west shore, somehow exudes the air of a seaside village even though the beach is a ten-minute walk from the centre. At the pebbly lakeshore you can feed the ducks, admire the ducklings, rent a boat or paddle in the lake.

For hikers there is a strenuous two-mile climb up Coniston Old Man, while gentler walks from jetty to jetty around the lake can be taken in conjunction with the launches.

GETTING to CONISTON
Bus 505 d. Ambleside for Coniston via Hawkshead Mo-Sa 1/hr;
Su every 1-2 hr (36 min)
Alight at either the Waterhead Ho-

Coniston Water from Brantwood

tel (Coniston, not on Windermere) for a short walk to the Coniston Launch, or in Coniston village centre for the Ruskin Museum, shops and a 10-minute walk to Coniston pier for the Coniston Launch and the Gondola. *Motion Sickness Alert!* The bus trip is very pretty, but there are a lot of curves and frequent sudden stops.

The Coniston Launches

Northern Cruise from Coniston Pier hourly. Round trip 50 min
Cost: A £4.60/Ch £2.30
Southern Cruise from Coniston Pier every two hours. Round trip 1½ hr
Cost: A £6.80/Ch £3.40
Dogs, bicycles and large push-chairs 50p. Discount for Brantwood. Flat-coated Retrievers travel free. Single fares are also available
Discount of 10% for YHA
Tel. 015394 36216
W: www.conistonlaunch.co.uk

Coniston Launch operates two traditional timber passenger boats: M.L. *Ransome* and M.L. *Ruskin*. These smooth, quiet boats are powered by electric motors that run off a combination of solar power and generator. They are the first U.K. commercial passenger boats operating on lochs and lakes to gain a Passenger Certificate using solar-electric power.

The **Northern Service** stops at Waterhead Hotel, Monk Coniston, Torver and Brantwood House. The

Southern Service includes the site of the *Bluebird* water speed attempt, "Wildcat Island", Brantwood House and jetties along the southern shores of the lake.

Steam Yacht *Gondola* (NT)

Departs Coniston Pier hourly from 11.00 (12.00 on Sa), excl. 13.00, d. Brantwood 35 min later.
Cost: Round trip A £5.80/Ch £2.80
No discount for NT members.
50p discount for Brantwood and Ruskin Museum. Reservations are recommended.
Tel. 015394 41288
E: regon@smtp.ntrust.org.uk

Gondola was launched in 1859 to carry passengers from the Furness Railway. She was retired in 1936 but revived as a houseboat in 1945 and remained as such until the sixties, when a storm tossed her onto the beach.

She was left derelict until rescued by the National Trust, rebuilt by Vickers Shipbuilding and relaunched in 1985. She is now used for cruises and private events, as befits her refurbished Victorian splendour.

Brantwood

Open daily 11.00-17.30
Cost: A £5.50/Co £4.00/Ch £1.00
Gardens only: £3.75
Tel. 015394 41396
W: www.brantwood.org.uk

John Ruskin was an artist, art critic, writer, reformer and philosopher who influenced such people as Gandhi, Oscar Wilde, Tolstoy, Marcel Proust and Frank Lloyd Wright.

The House

If the total of your Ruskin knowledge is based on the previous paragraph, the interesting introductory video will fill in the gaps, so keep an ear out for when the staff walk through the rooms announcing the next sitting.

Although most of the furniture, paintings and objects are original to the house, the effect is not exactly home-like. Rather, you are visiting a museum of sketches and watercolours by Ruskin and his contemporaries, with a fair number of Turner reproductions as well.

After Blackwell, the house itself may be a disappointment, but for those interested in Ruskin or in watercolours of his period, then Brantwood is a place to visit.

A handy little guide to the house is included in the entry fee.

The Gardens

These are quite special. Designed to create an idyllic country garden and woodland, they deliver some lovely surprises. The terraced gardens, for example, are laid out on a steep hill laced with twisting paths that could be used for a game of snakes and ladders.

Included in the entry fee is a map and a set of information cards, one for each garden, packaged in a waterproof cover. There are a lot of gardens spread over 250 acres so the map is particularly useful.

The Zig Zaggy garden must be started from the bottom (in the car park) and the description is definitely helpful as the whole is an allegorical journey from the gates of purgatory through the seven deadly sins to paradise! It would be very depressing to start at the top.

GOOD EATING

The Jumping Jenny uses local produce and on-site cooking to produce excellent lunches and teas. At peak times the queue is long and the service slow.

Return to Coniston via the launch, which departs hourly. (5 min)

Ruskin Museum

Open daily 10.00-17.30
Cost: A £3.75/Ch £1.75
50p discount for YHA.
With museum ticket, 50p off Adult Return or Single to Brantwood on the *Gondola*.
Tel. 015394 41164
W: www.ruskinmuseum.com

There are comprehensive exhibits on Ruskin, Donald Campbell and Bluebird, the geology of Coniston Old Man and local history. Local industries such as violin manufacture, wood carving and Ruskin pottery are represented by smaller displays, and there is an exquisite collection of Ruskin lace.

Base: Keswick

The market town of Keswick is larger and busier than Ambleside and is the centre for walking in the northern Lake District. It doesn't seem very promising when you arrive at the bus station, but take heart, you can be well into the hills a few minutes' walk from the town centre.

GETTING to KESWICK
Bus 555 d. Ambleside for Keswick Mo-Su 1/hr (40 min)
OR
Mainline rail station: PENRITH

RETURN to AMBLESIDE
Bus 505 d. Coniston for Ambleside via Hawkshead, Mo-Sa 1/hr; Su every 1-2 hr (35 min)

Bus X4, X5 d. Penrith rail stn for Keswick bus stn Mo-Sa 1/hr, Su every 2 hr (35 min)

From the bus station, turn left, and, in about 100 yards, turn right into Main Street and continue to the cobbled market place. Keswick's landmark, the Moot Hall, is at the far end. The TIC is at the back of the Moot Hall and provides town plans and walking maps. Derwentwater is a five- to ten-minute walk from the TIC.

GETTING to DERWENTWATER

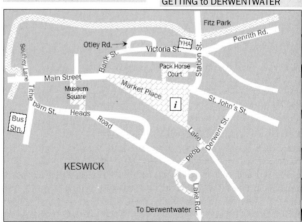

From the TIC take the pedestrian street that is a continuation of the right side of the market place and follow as it turns right into Lake Road. Cross the busy Heads Road by the underpass, then follow the footpath through the attractive gardens of Hope Park. These will take you to the tastefully developed lakeside promenade and Theatre by the Lake.

More rustic is the gently rolling field of Crow Park, which is visible from Lake Road. Owned by the National Trust and inhabited by sheep, it is a lovely place for a picnic and a paddle.

A pleasant expedition for your first evening is the easy stroll through rooky Castlehead Wood to a fine view over Derwentwater.

GETTING to the VIEWPOINT
From the TIC take St. John's Street. After it changes to Ambleside Road, start looking out for Springs Road on the right. About 170 yards along Springs Road look to your right for the footpath to Castlehead.

Activities on Derwentwater

Keswick Launches depart Keswick every half-hour (alternating between clockwise and anticlockwise) and call at six jetties around the lake. The round trip takes 50 minutes and costs £6.00 for adults and £3.00 for children.

One-way tickets are also available.

Rowing, sailing and small power boats are available for hire at several places at the north end of Derwentwater.

Canoes, kayaks, sail boats, dragon boats and power boats are available, with lessons, at **Platty+** near the ferry landing at Lodore.
Tel. 017687 76572
or 017687 77282
W: www.plattyplus.co.uk

While on the water keep an eye out for a flotilla of red squirrels paddling on tiny rafts to St. Herbert's Island. You might catch a glimpse of Squirrel Nutkin!

Fell Walking from Keswick

Keswick is surrounded by fells suitable for all levels of fitness and enthusiasm. The TIC has plenty of books and leaflets of local hikes and walks, but, if you want to do more than just walk around the lake, the best thing is to plan your hikes using the Ordnance Survey 1:25,000 map.

A moderate hike to the north of Keswick takes you up Latrigg (1,204 feet), while a serious hike goes up Skiddaw (3,053 feet). South-west of Keswick is Cat Bells (1,480 feet) accessed by the Keswick Launch to Hawes End.

Ashness Bridge, a local beauty spot, may be reached by a lakeside and woodland walk from Keswick or via Keswick Launch to Ashness Gate. The attractive bridge is made without mortar, like the drystone walls of the area.

Helvellyn, England's third highest peak at 3,118 feet, is a mildly prestigious one for the reasonably fit average walker to bag. The shortest route starts from Swirls car park, 10 minutes from Keswick by bus 555. The walking distance is about five miles and the actual climb is 2,460 feet.

The complete Helvellyn experience, incorporating Striding Edge and Swirral Edge, requires an approach from Glenridding (see page 181).

The Town

Keswick offers the usual range of craft shops and galleries, a large number of walking shops and several museums. Market day is Saturday.

Cars of the Stars Motor Museum

Open daily 10.00-17.00
Cost: A £4.00/Ch £3.00
Tel. 017687 73757

Features TV and film vehicles, such as the James Bond Aston Martin, the Batmobile and the Flintsones' Collection. Located opposite the far end of Packhorse Court.

Cumberland Pencil Museum

Open daily 9.30-16.00
Cost: A £3.00/Co £1.50-£2.00
Tel. 017687 73626
W: www.pencils.co.uk

Keswick is the home of the pencil-making industry and uses the best graphite in the world – Borrowdale. This museum describes the manufacturing process from mining the slate to the finished product. Children especially enjoy it. Located off Main Street just past Southey Lane.

Keswick Museum & Art Gallery

Open Good Friday-Oct, Tu-Sa, BH 10.00-16.00
Cost: Free
Tel. 017687 73263
W: www.allerdale.gov.uk/
keswick-museum

Located in Fitz Park, which offers bowls and tennis, the museum covers natural and social history and Lakes-oriented artwork.

Keswick Mining Museum

Open Tu-Su/BH 10.00-17.00
Cost: A £3.00/Ch £1.50
Tel. 017687 80055
E: coppermaid@aol.com
www.keswickminingmuseum.co.uk

This fascinating little museum is packed with a wide range of geological specimens, mining tools, photographs and interesting and evocative memorabilia. And, thank goodness, there is not an interactive computer in sight. You can even pan for gold.

The shop has one of the largest collections of mining and geology books in the county, as well as tools, gemstones and figures made from coal.

This is a good place to visit for an introduction to local mining before visiting the Honister Slate Mine. Located on the corner of Bank Street and Otley Road.

The Puzzling Place

Open daily 10.00-18.00
Cost: A £3.00/ Ch £2.50
Tel. 017687 75102
W. www.puzzlingplace.co.uk

The place to go if you like optical illusions, holograms and the like. Located in Museum Square.

Castlerigg Stone Circle (EH)

Unlimited access; Cost Free

Castlerigg stone circle may not be as spectacular as Stonehenge, but its setting is hard to beat. The circle is 100 feet in diameter and consists of 38 irregularly shaped stones that enclose a rectangle formed by another ten stones. The tallest stone is about eight feet high.

Nobody really knows what it is for, but it has been noted that the tallest stone lines up with Skiddaw and the setting sun at the summer solstice and with High Rigg and the rising sun at Candlemass in February. What's more, the views are terrific. The circle dates from about 3000BC.

GETTING to CASTLERIGG
SHORT WALK: From the TIC take the left exit from the wide end of the market square and almost immediately turn left into Station Road. Continue over the bridge and through Fitz Park until just before the road ends at the Keswick Hotel. Just as the road curves to the right, you should pick up the Railway Line Foot/Cycleway to Threlkeld on the left.

Follow the path across the river and continue until it goes under a road (the A591). Turn right along the A591 and follow the road as it turns left, signposted for A66, Threlkeld and Penrith. Don't continue on the A591 to Ambleside!

In about 160 yards turn down the lane on the right. You will eventually see the stone circle in a field on the right. Distance is about 1½ miles east of Keswick; 1 mile after leaving the Foot/Cycleway.

BUS 86 d. Keswick bus stn Mo-Sa 1/day. Allows 18 min at Castlerigg.

Bus 73, 73A d. Keswick bus stn Apr, May, Sep, Oct on Sa only; Jun, Jul on Sa, Su/BH; Aug Mo-Su. 1/day. Allows 55 min at Castlerigg in conjunction with Bus 86 for return to Keswick.

Castlerigg is also accessible by a longer, scenic walk on footpaths through woods and fields. A descriptive leaflet is available at the TIC.

BASE: KESWICK
Honister Pass and Buttermere (half or full day)

GETTING THERE
Bus 77A d. Keswick bus stn and completes a circular route via Portinscale, Catbells, Grange Bridge, Seatoller, Honister, Buttermere, Lorton and Whinlatter Mo-Su 4/day (1½ hr round trip). Bus 77 follows the same route in reverse Mo-Su 4/day (1½ hr).
Motion Sickness Alert!

This bus trip takes in some spectacular scenery: the bleak slates of Honister, the green fields and trees of Buttermere and the deep blue-green of Crummock Water. The non-stop round trip takes just over 1½ hours, but much better is to spread it over the day by stopping at Honister Slate Mine and Buttermere.

Many hikers take the first bus of the day, so arrive at the bus station at least ten minutes early to join the queue. An overloaded bus won't get over Honister Pass!

Honister Slate Mine
Open Mo-Fr 9.00-17.00
Sa & Su 10.00-17.00
Tours at 10.30, 12.30 and 15.30
Cost: A £9.50/Ch £4.50

Reservations are essential
Tel. 017687 77230
W: www.honister-slate-mine.co.uk

About 500 years ago the monks (or, more likely, the lay brothers and servants) of Furness Abbey (see Tour 6, page 207) started digging for the characteristic Borrowdale green slate within Fleetwith Pike at Honister Pass. The slate is mined here still.

Honister Slate Mine is open to the public with guided tours into the mine, around the edge of the mountain "if you dare" and into the workshop where you can try working some slate yourself. Tours last about 1¾ hour. **Reservations are essential** – telephone the above number. There is also a visitor centre with a café and shop.

Warm clothes and stout shoes are recommended. The necessary safety equipment is provided. Children under 8 years are prohibited from the Edge Tour.

Buttermere
Both Buttermere and Crummock Water are owned by the National Trust, as is much of the surround-

ing land. There is a 4½- mile walk around Buttermere and a two-mile walk along the south-western edge of Crummock Water to reach the 125-foot waterfall Scale Force. There are many picnic spots and boats are available for hire.

BASE: KESWICK
Day Trip to Cockermouth

To see everything it is necessary to visit on Monday, Tuesday, Wednesday or Thursday. The Lakeland Sheep show is closed Friday and Saturday, Wordsworth House on Sunday and the Brewery on Saturday and Sunday.

Cockermouth is another Wordsworth port of call: the National Trust owns the house where he was born and spent his early years. The town also has a splendid toy and model museum (which, at the time of going to press, was under threat of closure due to lack of funds), a brewery tour (with three free half-pints!) and a sheep show with a sheepdog demonstration.

To top it off, the bus route passes Bassenthwaite Lake on one shore going out and the opposite coming back. The scenery is varied with miniature mountains plopped down in the middle of soft green fields – quite beautiful.

The whole makes an enjoyable and interesting day out if planned ahead. The important thing is to co-ordinate the sheep show with the brewery tour! Plan to watch the 10.30 Sheep Show, visit Wordsworth's house, pause for lunch then take the 14.00 Brewery Tour. The toy museum, if still open, is a fine finish to the day.

GETTING to COCKERMOUTH
Buses X4/X5 d. Keswick bus stn for Cockermouth Mo-Sa 1/hr (on alternating hours); Su (X5 only) every 2 hr (30 min) Alight at Cockermouth town centre.
X4 goes north-east of Bassenthwaite; X5, south-west.

Lakeland Sheep and Wool Centre

Open daily 9.00-17.30
Sheep Show Su-Th 10.30, 12.00, 14.00 and 15.30.
Cost: General admission free
Sheep Show A £4.00/Ch £3.00
Tel. 01900 822 673
W: www.sheep-woolcentre.co.uk

GETTING to THE SHEEP & WOOL CENTRE
From the town centre bus stop walk back to Station Road and turn right. Follow the road to the busy intersection with Gallowbarrow on the right and Fern Bank on the left. Station Road does a bit of

a jog left then right and becomes The Level.

There should be a school playing field on the left. Follow the road that hugs the playing field and turn left into Mountain View, which becomes Skiddaw View then Lamplugh Road. Keep following Lamplugh Road to the roundabout junction of the A66 and A5086.

Go straight across the roundabout and the entrance to the Lakeland Sheep and Wool Centre is about 200 yards on the left (20-25 min).

The Lakeland Sheep and Wool Centre is primarily a large woollen-products shop. There is a mildly interesting exhibition of the western lakes, but it isn't worth the twenty-minute walk if you aren't also interested in buying Lakeland woollies.

What makes the visit worthwhile is the **Sheep Show**.

The sheep have been trained for this and their individual characters shine through – the whole is both entertaining and interesting. You get to see sheepdogs at work, always a fascinating experience, and, in season, a shearing display. The show lasts about 30 minutes, or a bit longer if there are lots of questions.

There are no Sheep Shows on Friday or Saturday.

Wordsworth House (NT)
Open Mo-Sa 11.00-16.30 by timed ticket
Cost: A £4.50/Ch £2.50
Tel. 01900 820 882
or 01900 824805
E: wordsworthhouse
@nationaltrust.org.uk

From the bus stop cross Main Street, turn left and the house will soon appear on the right.

This 1745 Georgian townhouse is the birthplace of William Wordsworth (7 April 1770) and his sister Dorothy (25 December 1771).

Their parents, Anne and John, married and moved into the house in 1766. The impression is that of a happy home, crowded with five children, but Anne died in 1778 and John five years later. The children were sent to relatives.

"Hands-off" rooms contain period furniture, while others contain modern replicas where "hands-on" is positively encouraged.

Children can try on costumes while adults rummage through the drawers. There is often cooking in the kitchen and volunteers in period costume role-play as appropriate to their station in life. An excellent leaflet is provided and friendly staff and servants happily answer your questions. Allow 30 to 45 minutes for your visit.

Jennings Brewery Tour

Open Shop Mo-Fr 9.00-17.00
Sa (and Su in Jul, Aug) 10.00-
16.00
Tours Mo-Fr at 11.00 and 14.00
Cost: A £4.95/Ch £2.00 (must be
over 12 yrs) Advance booking is
essential.
Tel. 0845 1297 190
W: www.jenningsbrewery.co.uk

From the bus stop cross Main Street and turn right. Take the first left into High Sand Lane and follow the path over the bridge, to the right and on to the brewery.

The guided tour lasts about 1½ hours and includes a tasting session in the traditional-style bar. The cost of admission includes three half-pints or a generous sample of each Jennings beer.

The beer-making process is explained on the tour. There are quite a few stairs to climb and the smell is a bit heady! A must for would-be ale connoisseurs and anyone unsure of the difference between lager and bitter.

The Cumberland Toy and Model Museum

Open daily 10.00-17.00
Cost: A £3.00/Co £2.60/Ch £1.50
Tel. 01900 827606
E: rod@toymuseum.co.uk
W: www.toymuseum.co.uk

Leave Jennings Brewery by the main gate into Wyndham Row.

There is a castle (not open to the public) on the hill to the left. Turn right into Castle Gate back toward the town centre and very soon on your right will be a sign pointing down a narrow alley to the museum.

This treasure chest of toys and models is located in old industrial buildings on one side of a tiny court. Inside is like the attic of an idyllic childhood home – if you see nothing from your own childhood you can't have spent it in the Commonwealth, or at least in Britain: Bayko™ sets, puppets, costume dolls, all sorts of Meccano™ gadgets, train sets and anything else you can imagine.

Several gadgets work by push-button: some for 10p, some free. The money helps maintain the toys and the rest goes to Mountain Rescue. This is a place not to miss.

At time of going to press, this museum was under threat of closure.

RETURN to KESWICK
Bus X4, X5 d. Cockermouth Main Street 1/hr. Su (X5 only) every 2 hr (30 min). If you took bus X4 to Cockermouth, try to take X5 back to Keswick, and vice versa, thus seeing the greatest variety of scenery.

Base: Glenridding for Ullswater and Helvellyn

It is by the shore of Ullswater that Wordsworth "...saw a crowd, a host of golden daffodils." In April you can see them too.

At the south-west end of Ullswater is Glenridding, a slatey village with a dramatic backdrop of Cumbrian mountains. From Glenridding you can climb Helvellyn; walk the eight-mile round trip to Aira Force, a waterfall renowned as a beauty spot since Victorian times; or spend a day on the lake exploring from each pier.

Plan ahead to get the most out of your stay in this lovely area.

GETTING to GLENRIDDING
Bus X4, X5 d. Keswick bus stn for Penrith bus station Mo-Sa 1/hr; Su every 2 hr (40 min).

Bus 108 d. Penrith bus station for Pooley Bridge (ask for the Ullswater Launch, which is on the far side of Pooley Bridge) (20 min) and Glenridding (40 min) Mo-Sa every 2 hr; Su every 2-3 hr

ULLSWATER STEAMERS
Runs Mo-Su but frequency depends on season. Timetables available at TICs and website.
Cost (return) Pooley Bridge to Glenridding: A £9.80/Ch £4.90
Tel. 017684 82229
W: www.ullswater-steamers.co.uk

The Ullswater Launch stops at Pooley Bridge, Howtown and Glenridding. The pier houses at Pooley Bridge and Glenridding offer light lunches and snacks as well as toilets and splendid views.

The pier house shops also sell

Ullswater from Helvellyn

"Walks for All" leaflets that describe some of the walks that connect with the steamers. These range from short circular walks to longer hikes from pier to pier.

Aira Force (NT)
Unlimited access; Cost free
Tel. 017684 82067
E: ullswater@nationaltrust.org.uk

The road from Glenridding is very busy and narrow so walking along it is not advisable. Contact the National Trust for their walks leaflet. Alternatively, take Bus 108 from Glenridding to Park Brow Foot (seven minutes) and walk from there.

Overnight in Glenridding.

Helvellyn Hike

Helvellyn is the most climbed mountain in England; the path is hard to miss, but don't let that trick you into a false sense of security. Please read Tips for Safe Hiking on page 183.

If you stay at the youth hostel you will have a head start on the hike (and a very good evening meal). The hostel has a scale model of the area so you can get a good idea of where you are going.

Striding Edge

The classic route is up Striding Edge and down Swirral Edge. Don't forget to ask for a packed lunch.

No matter how calm and sunny the day, Striding Edge needs to be taken very seriously. This doesn't mean you need special equipment or skills: good hiking boots, reasonable fitness and common sense are the basic requirements, but the top is narrow, the sides steep and the end of a tumble is a very long way down. If you try to stay on the peak, you will find yourself negotiating something a bit wider than a tightrope but much less smooth and stable.

The path just below the peak on the north side (Red Tarn side) is generally easier, but is not always there, so you still have to do some scrambling. If this is your first mountain walk, are the least afraid of heights, or are a bit unsteady on your legs, Striding Edge will probably be a nightmare. You can always take the easier route from Keswick (see page 174).

The route from Glenridding past the youth hostel to Red Tarn, along Striding Edge to the top of Helvellyn, down Swirral Edge and back to the village will take about six hours, including a lunch break on top.

Getting Home

Bus 108 d. Glenridding and Pooley Bridge for Penrith Mo-Sa every 2 hours; Su every 2-3 hours. The bus stops at Penrith mainline railway station from where you can head north or south.

Tips for Safe Hiking

The Country Code

The following guidelines help ensure the well-being of the land, the inhabitants and the visitors:

- Be safe – plan ahead and follow any signs
- Leave gates and property as you find them
- Protect plants and animals and take your litter home
- Keep dogs under close control
- Consider other people

Safe walking

Never underestimate the changeability of English weather and the treachery of the terrain. These tips will help keep you out of difficulty on off-road walks or hikes.

- Take extra sweaters and water- and wind-proof jacket and trousers
- Wear good hiking boots or strong walking shoes
- A 1:25,000 Ordnance Survey map is useful on short walks and essential on longer ones, but only if you can read it! The same applies to a compass.
- Take water and food. I always carry a supply of chocolate-covered Kendal Mint Cake. Hunger, fatigue and dehydration lead to accidents.

- Carry a whistle and a reflective emergency blanket that folds to fit into a pocket.
- Tell someone your route and when you expect to return. Report in when you do return or if you are late but safe. Mountain rescue teams are not too thrilled searching for "casualties" found happily ensconced with a pie and a pint.

On rougher terrain

- Do not get tired – you will get clumsy and may trip. Go at your own pace.
- Look where you put your feet. Stop, then admire the view!
- Even large rocks can be unsteady. Test it before you trust it. This applies to handholds and footholds.
- Do not run downhill.
- Do not take unnecessary risks. If you injure yourself you will inconvenience and put at risk a lot of other people.

If you show proper respect for the hills, the weather and your own limitations, you are very unlikely to come to any harm.

Highlights of Tour 6

- Mainline Rail Station: Carlisle
  - **Whitehaven:** Maryport, St. Bees, The Rum Story, mining, maritime and Roman museums, bird watching, beaches
  - **Ravenglass:** Sellafield, Muncaster Castle, miniature railway to Eskdale
  - **Wasdale/Wasdale Head:** hike to Wastwater
  - **Ulverston:** Holker Hall, Cartmel, Furness Abbey, Wild Animal Park
- Mainline Rail Station: Lancaster or Manchester

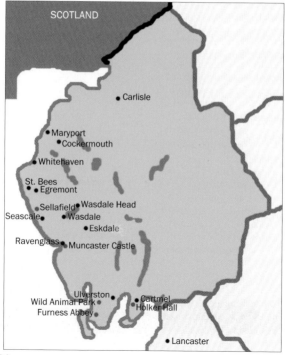

Tour 6 – The Cumbrian Coast

The coast of Cumbria has long been something of a poor cousin to the Lake District. The prosperity of its towns was based on mining and fishing, vital industries in their time, but not exactly attractive and now essentially defunct. The decay born of redundancy gave the area a reputation for grim dreariness that still persists – unfairly, as it happens.

The tour starts at Carlisle and heads to the coast at Whitehaven from where a day trip to Maryport is possible. Both are lively and attractive seaside towns, proud of their past and providing much to see and do in the present.

Further south is the pleasingly unusual tributary village of Ravenglass. Bleak on a rainy day it may be, but an uplifting, wild sort of bleakness based on sand dunes, salt water and wind.

Inland a little, a similar aura wraps around Wastwater and Scafell Pike, the deepest lake and highest mountain in England.

South again is Ulverston, home of the Laurel & Hardy Museum. This market and festival town makes a convenient base for trips to the awesome remains of Furness Abbey and to Cartmel, home of the best sticky toffee pudding in England.

There's more: Roman remains, stately homes and gardens, wild animals and birds of prey. All those sand dunes and tributaries make the area a bird-watcher's paradise and there's whale-watching, too. For technophiles there are coal and iron mining museums, a motor museum, wind farms galore and infamous Sellafield, the site of the nuclear power station called Windscale (now out of operation), and a uranium reprocessing plant.

So give the coast of Cumbria a try. For variety it's hard to beat!

Chimneys of Whitehaven

Accommodation (see page 10 for abbreviations)

WHITEHAVEN, Cumbria – 2 nights
Glenard Guest House, Inkerman Terrace, Whitehaven CA28 7TY
Tel. 01946 692 249
E: glenard@uk-business-search.co.uk   W: www.glenard.co.uk
Rooms (£pppn): 2Ss, 2Ds, 2Ts, 2Fs (£20)

Lismore Guest House, 28 Wellington Row, Whitehaven CA28 7HE
Tel. 01946 66028; E: pamcliffdixon@btopenworld.com
Rooms (£pppn): 1Ss, 1Ds, 3Ts, 1Fs (£20-£21)

The Cottage B&B, Mirehouse Road, Whitehaven CA28 9UD
Tel. 01946 695 820
Rooms (£pppn): 3S/T/D of which 2 can be F, 2e (£20)
Outside Whitehaven but convenient for bus. Bus 4 or 5 d. Whitehaven Duke Street for Mirehouse Shops (11 min). Follow the road
with the shops on your left, cross the railway bridge and immediately
turn left down the narrow footpath. After about 100 yards is a busy
road with a large brick barn on the far side. Cross the road into the
barnyard. The B&B is the white building (5-10 min walk).

RAVENGLASS , Cumbria – 1 night
Rose Garth Guest House, Main Street, Ravenglass CA18 1SQ
Tel. 01229 717 275
E: rosegarth1@yahoo.co.uk   W: www.rosegarth1.fsnet.co.uk
Rooms (£pppn) 1Se, 1Te, 3De, 1Fe (£23.00), S in D £30.00

Holly House Hotel, Main Street, Ravenglass CA18 1SQ
Tel 01229 717 230; W: www.thehollyhousehotel.com
Rooms (£pppn): 1Ss, 1Ts (£22); 2De (£25); 2Fe (£70/room);
S in D £30

*Muncaster Country Guest House, Ravenglass CA18 1RD
Tel: 01229 717 693
E: ronandjan@muncastercountryguesthouse.com
W: www.muncastercountryguesthouse.co.uk
Rooms (£/room): 2Ss (£25); 1Ts, 1Ds (£45); 2De (£50);
1F es (varies). Will collect from Ravenglass rail station

*The Coachman's Quarters, Muncaster Castle, Ravenglass
CA18 1RQ   Tel. 01229 717 614
E: info@muncaster.co.uk   W: www.muncaster.co.uk
Rooms (£/room): 8Te/De, 1Tpb/Dpb (£65.00); S in D £35.00

*Muncaster is a little under two miles from the rail station at Ravenglass. There is a bus service from Whitehaven to Muncaster via Ravenglass that runs Mo-Su three times a day (4 on Sa) . Details are provided in the itinerary for Days 3 and 4, pages 199 and 201.

WASDALE and WASDALE HEAD, Cumbria – 1 night

YHA, Wasdale Hall, Wasdale CA20 1ET
Tel. 0870 770 6082; Int (+44) 019467 26222
E: wastwater@yha.org.uk
Cost £11.00/£8.00
Open: Flexible. Jul & Aug daily; Rec. 8.00-10.00, 17.00-22.00
Good homemade food, including the bread.

Wasdale Head Inn, Wasdale Head CA20 1EX
Tel. 019467 26229
E: wasdaleheadinn@msn.com   W: www.wasdale.com
Rooms (£pppn): 2Se, 4Te, 6De (£49-£69)

Burnthwaite Farm, Wasdale Head CA20 1EX
Tel. 019467 26242; E: burnthwaite123@aol.com
Rooms (£pppn) 1Ss, 3Ts, 1Ds (£25); 1Te, 1De (£30)
As you approach Wasdale Head follow the right side of the roughly triangular green to Ingfell House. Follow the lane on the left of the house to the farm. A National Trust farm with beautiful drystone walls, contented cattle, sheep, sheep dogs, house dogs, barn cats and house cats. The baths are long and have plenty of hot water. Highly recommended.

ULVERSTON, Cumbria – 2 nights

Sefton House, 34 Queen Street, Ulverston LA12 7AF
Tel. 01229 582 190
E: usrunner@btopenworld.com   W: www.seftonhouse.co.uk
Rooms (£/room): 1Ss (£30); 1Ts, 1Ds, 2De (£50); 1Fe (£60)

The Walkers Hostel, Oubas Hill, Ulverston LA12 7LB
Tel. 01229 585 588; E: povey@walkershostel.co.uk
Rooms (£pppn) 2- to 7-bedded £14 B&B

Rock House, 1 Alexander Road, Ulverston LA12 0DE
Tel. 01229 586 879; E: ian@rock-house.info
Rooms (£pppn) 1Ss, 2Fs (£25); 1Fe (£35)

Days 1 & 2 – In and Around Whitehaven

The Georgian town of Whitehaven has the oldest harbour in Cumbria, but don't call it a harbour: it's gone all upscale and is now referred to as The Marina.

Whitehaven has enough museums and sights to fill a day, rain or shine. It is ideally located for day trips to Maryport for the aquarium, Maritime museum and Roman museum; St. Bees for birds, cliffs and beaches; and Egremont for the Florence Mine Heritage Centre.

GETTING to WHITEHAVEN
Mainline rail station: CARLISLE
For more information on Carlisle see page 141.

Train d. Carlisle for Whitehaven Mo-Sa every ¾-1¾ hr; Su 3/day in p.m. & evening (67 min)

St. Nicholas Tower Chapel and Gardens

The first chapel on this site was built in 1642. This was a time of rapid population growth in Whitehaven, so the chapel was soon replaced by a larger church which was itself replaced in 1883. When this, the third church, burned in 1971 the parish authorities decided to turn the site into a place for quiet reflection.

The surviving tower houses a chapel and a peaceful café, while

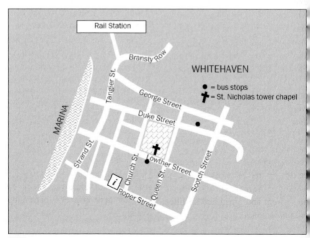

the broken walls of the nave have been incorporated into a thoughtful memorial garden. There is a fascinating collection of unusual plants and trees, including the bizarrely inevitable huddle of sad palms wistfully dreaming, it always seems to me, of far more tropical climes. A single flowering tree has been dedicated to all victims of war.

A mosaic set in the nave floor shows a pit wheel with the names of the coal mines that operated near Whitehaven from 1597 to 1986, when the last mine closed, listed on the spokes.

At the far end of the park, furthest from the chapel, is a small, exquisite memorial to the children who died in the pits between 1813 and 1915. The youngest were eight years old: Abraham Taylor, died 12 November 1831 and William Savage, died 2 August 1839.

The sculpture includes a pit pony: a reminder that they, too, were exploited in the cause of industry.

The gardens are very beautiful and succeed in touching the heart. It is appropriate that a space dedicated to those who lived and worked in the noise and dark should be so light and green and so filled with birdsong.

The Rum Story

Open daily 10.00-17.00 (16.00 in Oct)
Cost: A £4.95/Co £3.95/Ch £2.95
There is a significant reduction if you buy a joint ticket for The Rum Story and The Beacon.
Tel. 01946 592 933
W: www.rumstory.co.uk

Located in the premises of the Jefferson family business, The Rum Story is fascinating, entertaining and disturbing.

The history and making of rum are described through text and videos as you walk through tableaux of tropical forests, ships' holds and smugglers' caves to the office and warehouse.

At the heart of the rum story are slaves. Their tragedy is depicted with an appropriately distressing realism.

On a lighter note, keep an eye out for Henry, the mischievous resident ghost and, as you exit, test your new-found knowledge on a free sample of Jefferson's rum.

GOOD EATING

The Courtyard Café at The Rum Story provides an excellent range of salads at a very reasonable price, as well as the usual jacket potatoes and sandwiches. Time your visit to arrive in the courtyard at noon to watch the kinetic clock act out the story of rum-making as it strikes twelve.

This you *can* believe!

The Beacon

Open Tu-Su/BH/SH 10.00-17.30
Cost: A £4.40/Co £3.60/Ch £2.90
There is a significant reduction if you buy a joint ticket for The Rum Story and The Beacon.
Tel. 01946 592 302
W: www.copelandbc.gov.uk/ms/www/thebeacon

The Beacon contains three compact storeys of tableaux, videos and audio recordings relating Whitehaven's colourful history of rum, smuggling and mining.

The top storey is the Met Office Weather Gallery, a fun place to learn about weather, climate and micro-climates.

The Haig Colliery Mining Museum

Open daily 9.30-16.30
Cost: free
Tel. 01946 599 949
W: www.haigpit.com

GETTING THERE
View with grave suspicion all pedestrian and road signs for the museum. They will lead you on an infuriating hike to Kells (not the one in Ireland, although it feels like it) and back again as you curse the idiot who described the museum's location as "only a twenty-minute stroll from Whitehaven Harbour".

Actually, it really is a twenty-minute stroll from the harbour, but not if you follow the signs!

Here are the real directions.

From The Beacon go up the long flight of steps on your right and turn right at the top. Walk toward the coast, onto a footpath that soon turns left to follow the shore-line.

About here there is a sign saying "COASTAL FOOTPATH Haig mining museum 700 yards". That one you can believe. The path goes up more steps but then levels out. Look back for some fine views over the Solway.

Continue with the sea on your right. You will soon see a big brick building to your left (see photograph on page 5). Follow the signs and don't be alarmed when you climb the final ramp to find a closed solid wooden door without so much as a "Museum" sign on it. Enter and you are there.

Housed in the engine room of Haig Pit, which was purchased by the Haig Pit Restoration Group for £1.00, this delightfully old-fashioned museum tells its story with creased photographs, written recollections and worn mining tools. Lacking, as it does, the videos and computer interactivity of more "child-friendly" museums, the collection is heavier to swallow than those, but its impact is stronger. Its strength is in the details and, if you make the effort, you will soon be absorbed in the lives of the mining community.

The second room houses large machinery, and entry is only permitted with a guide. If no one seems to be around try shouting "Hello!", and see what happens.

◈ Author's Rant ◈

Why did Whitehaven choose to pardon, in 1999, John Paul Jones – a man who sailed for several years on a slave ship, who fled when accused of murdering a mutineer, who turned traitor and fought for the American navy and finally led an attack on Whitehaven, the town where he had served his apprenticeship?

Option – Full day in Maryport

Maryport is another Georgian town with a long and honourable seafaring history. It offers a seaside promenade, an aquarium, a maritime museum and a Roman fort, as well as dramatic coastal views. There are pubs and fish & chip shops, and a family café at the Aquarium.

Note: Sunday is not a good day to visit – the train service is minimal, there is no bus service and the maritime museum is closed.

GETTING to MARYPORT
Train d. Whitehaven for Maryport
Mo-Sa every ¾-1¾ hr; Su 3/day
in p.m. & evening (28 min)
OR
Bus 30,30A d. Whitehaven Low-
ther St. for Maryport Curzon St.
Mo-Sa 3/hr (1 hr) No Su service

Lake District Coast Aquarium
Open daily 10.00-17.00
Cost: A £4.75/Ch £3.10
Tel. 01900 817 760
W: www.lakedistrict-coastaquarium
.co.uk

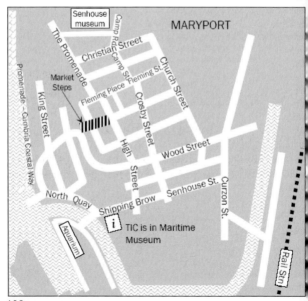

The aquarium is quite small but has a wide variety of weird fish from tiny baby seahorses to huge conger eels. You can stroke the skates, if you like that sort of thing, watch at feeding times (on the hour from noon to 16.00) and listen to pool-side talks.

Maryport Maritime Museum

Open Mo-Sa 10.00-16.00
Cost: free
Tel. 01900 813 738

This little museum is conveniently located in the TIC and is well worth a visit. It features in-depth displays on three local boys: founder of the White Star Line Thomas Henry Ismay, Captain Bligh of the *Bounty*, and his mutinous Master Mate Fletcher Christian.

Advertisements from the White Star Line and items from their ships present the joys of travel on luxury ocean liners, while quite a different life is depicted in the paintings, shipboard articles and logs from the *Bounty*.

Senhouse Roman Museum

Open Jul-Oct daily
Apr-Jun Tu,Th-Su/BH, 10.00-17.00
Cost: A £2.50/Ch 75p
Tel. 01900 816 168
W: www.senhousemuseum.co.uk

In AD122 the Emperor Hadrian ordered a fort and temple be built in Maryport as part of his northern defences. About 1,400 years later, John Senhouse began collecting artefacts from the same fort. Now the oldest antiquarian collection in Britain, his finds form the core of the Senhouse Roman Museum.

Children can participate in an archaeological dig, dress as Roman soldiers and follow their own guide book. From the viewing tower you can visualise the fort layout and enjoy a coastal vista.

At the command of Emperor Hadrian, Roman soldiers approach Maryport
©LEGIIAVG

RETURN to WHITEHAVEN	OR
Train d. Maryport for Whitehaven Mo-Sa every ¾-1¾ hr; Su 3/day in p.m. & evening (28 min)	Bus d. Maryport Curzon St. for Whitehaven Duke St. Mo-Sa 3/hr (1 hr) No Su service

Option – Full or half-day in St. Bees

St. Bees is the place to go for bird watching. The beach is good, too: a vast expense of sand at the foot of red sandstone cliffs that are the highest in England. Meals are served at a couple of hotels and pubs in the village, half a mile away, but a picnic is more appropriate for the locale.

There are no Sunday train or bus services to St. Bees.

GETTING to ST. BEES
Train d. Whitehaven for St. Bees Mo-Fr at irregular intervals of ¾-2½ hr; Sa every ¾-1¾ hr (8 min)

OR Bus 20 d. Whitehaven Duke St. for St. Bees beach and rail stn Mo-Sa 1/hr (exc 11:xx) (20 min)

St. Bees is named after Bega, an Irish girl who, around AD900, sailed to Cumbria alone to avoid marriage to a Viking chieftain.

Visible from the railway station are the remains of St. Bees' Priory. The church contains several ancient and interesting features: a shaft from a Viking cross, the 12thC west door, 13thC interior arches and columns, and the remains of "St. Bees' Man". Discovered in 1981, this unknown man's body had been wrapped in shroud and enclosed in lead, ensuring remarkable degree of preservation.

To get to the beach from the priory church backtrack a little towards the rail station and turn right into the footpath beside the school playing field. The path leads to a lane that angles slightly to the left and goes to the beach.

Keep the sea on your right until you reach a lane that doubles back uphill. The lane becomes a road to the village and back to the rail station. The circuit is about 2¼ miles.

St. Michael fights a dragon. Stone lintel (c. 1120) from St. Bees' Church

RETURN to WHITEHAVEN	Sa every ¾-1¾ hr (8 min)
Train d. St. Bees Mo-Fr at irregular intervals of ¾-2½ hr	Bus 20 d. St. Bees Beach Mo-Sa 1/hr (exc. 12:xx) (20 min)

Option – Half day at Florence Mine

If you have a serious and knowledgeable interest in the mining of iron then the Heritage Centre is for you. There are displays for a more general audience, but the centre is heavy on detailed technology. More exciting is the underground tour available by advance booking.

GETTING THERE

Bus 30/30A d. Whitehaven Duke St. for Egremont Mo-Sa 3/hr; Su 1/hr (25 min) Alight opposite Graham's Garage (just after Egremont), almost at the start of Little Mill lane. Follow the lane uphill and the mine centre will be on the right (5 min)

Florence Mine Heritage Centre
Open Mo-Fr 9.30-15.30
Sa,Su/BH 10.00-16.00
Cost: A £2.00/Ch £1.00
Tel. 01946 825 830
W: www.florencemine.co.uk
Underground tours Sa,Su/BH arrive at noon for 12:30 tour. Book in advance at Tel. 01946 820 683. Underground tours on weekdays are available by arrangement.
Tel. 01946 820 683

About Days 3 and 4

Wastwater is my favourite of the Cumbrian lakes. From the south-east, the Screes crack and slide to the bed of the deepest lake in England (260 feet) with scarcely a pause for a shoreline footpath. The water is black, the fells mist-shrouded. To the north-east is Scafell Pike, the highest mountain in England at 3,210 feet.

Getting there by public transport is simple – if you are up for an easy-to-moderate hike of about four hours (including Kendal Mint Cake breaks). This is described as Days 3A and 4A.

If you are not up for such a hike, there are two taxi-bus runs on each of Thursday, Saturday and Sunday that will get you there in style. This option is described as Days 3B and 4B.

Either way, you have the chance to stop off at the Sellafield Visitor Centre. Both options A and B include an overnight stay at Wasdale and at Ravenglass with time to visit Muncaster Castle.

About Wasdale

The Wasdale fells were belched forth by geological spasms then scoured with glacial force. The turmoil has settled, but the area retains the brooding look of a chronic dyspeptic, in spite of millennia of occupation.

Late stone age workers hacked at the crags of Scafell and hewed axe heads that were transported to the village of Gosforth for final polishing before being shipped to communities along the coast. These settlers scattered stone circles about the landscape.

Bronze Age farmers, who radically cleared the woodlands and left piled stone cairns, were followed by Romans with their roads, forts and ports.

When the Romans departed, the area was left in a peace unknown further east. Any Angles and Vikings that eventually washed up on

the coast of Cumbria came to escape the turmoil of their own making and settle to a life of farming. They completed the deforestation and cleared the valleys of stones, incorporating them into the characteristic massive walls of Wasdale: not of slate, as in the heart of the Lake District, but of rounded light-grey rock.

It is to the Viking King Olaf that the little church between Wasdale Head Inn and Burnthwaite Farm is dedicated. One of the smallest in England, it nestles among the trees and fades, stone to stone, into its surroundings.

The otherwise meticulous Normans, who recorded every landholding and chattel across Britain, left Wasdale out of the notorious Domesday Book.

It must have been this isolation that attracted a 15thC counterfeiter the 18thC smugglers and the 19thC poets and painters. Wordsworth and Coleridge got quite carried away, poetically speaking, or Scafell Pike, but the Romantic painters, for reasons best known to themselves, turned the already dramatic landscape into an unlikely fantasy of towering peaks and plummeting waterfalls. The mountains of Cumbria are all sorts of wonderful things, but towering they are not!

By the late nineteenth century, climbers had discovered that Scafell and Great Gable made excellent practice grounds for more serious climbing elsewhere. Sir Edmund Hillary, the first European to reach the summit of Everest, prepared here.

Wasdale Inn (Wordsworth stayed here when it was called The Huntsman's Inn) and Burnthwaite Farm are at Wasdale Head, at the foot of Great Gable at the north-east end of Wastwater.

The Youth Hostel is at Wasdale at the south-west end of the lake.

About Ravenglass

Ravenglass is an old fishing and smuggling village at the junction of the Rivers Irt, Mite and Esk. The rivers join forces and flow into the sea through a break in a wide expanse of sand dunes that form part of the Drigg Dunes and Irt Estuary Nature Reserve.

The area has been settled for at least 2,000 years, long enough for its name to have three possible derivations: fern-green (Irish), blue river (Celtic) and mouth of a river (Norse).

A hint of a contraband past is revealed at low tide. As you walk along the sand behind the houses look out for the flight of steps that lead from the water to – a blank wall. Make of that what you will.

The steel gates at the south end of the main street keep the sea out during particularly high tides.

Half a mile south of the village are the substantial remains of a Roman bath house, and a mile further on is Muncaster Castle with its fabulous gardens and World Owl Centre.

Because Ravenglass is small you will need to book a room early. The Holly House Hotel and Rose Garth Guest House are on the main street of Ravenglass facing the rivers.

If you are staying at the Muncaster Country Guest House or The Coachman's Quarters, there

Wasdale Head

is a pretty walking route to Muncaster or there is a bus from Ravenglass rail station. Refer to page 199 for directions.

GOOD EATING in RAVENGLASS

The **Rose Garth Tea Rooms** serve delightful home-cooked lunches and teas at a reasonable price. Open from 11.00-16.00. Opening days vary depending on the season.

Holly House Hotel serves excellent traditional food, including steak and ale pie, and really sticky toffee pudding with custard. Order at the bar. The bar area is smoky, but the dining room, which is hidden behind two doors, is a no-smoking area.

The Ratty Arms by the railway station is a large pub/restaurant, busier and noisier than the little pub at Holly House. The no-smoking area is smoke-reduced rather than smoke-free. The main courses are a little disappointing but the sweets are good.

Ravenglass & Eskdale Miniature Railway

Runs daily approximately hourly. Timetables are available at the station (next to the main rail station), guest houses and TICs in the area, and at the REMR web site.
Cost (Ravenglass to Eskdale)
return: A £8.60/Ch £4.30
one-way: A £5.30/Ch £2.60
Tel. 01229 717 171
W: www.ravenglass-railway.co.uk

Beside the mainline railway station is the lower terminus of the Ravenglass and Eskdale Miniature Railway (REMR – also known as La'al Ratty). This fifteen-inch gauge railway started life in 1871 as a three-foot gauge line used to carry iron ore and granite from the upland workings to the mainline station at Ravenglass.

The line closed in 1915, but W.J. Bassett-Lowke converted the tracks to carry his model engines. Now steam and diesel engines haul carriages of hikers and sightseers on a seven-mile, forty-minute journey through marshland and woods to Dalegarth at the foot of England's highest mountains. The pace is slow enough to look out for herons, deer and the rare red squirrels.

Within ten minutes' walk of Dalegarth are Boot, with its old packhorse bridge, and Eskdale Corn Mill, the oldest working water mill in England. There is a nice pub in Boot and a café in the station.

The history of the REMR is related in a little museum between the main and miniature rail lines at Ravenglass.

Roman Bath House (EH)
Open daily, unlimited access
Cost: free

198

The bath house is on the walking route to Muncaster Castle and is less than half a mile from the middle of Ravenglass. It can also be included in a one-mile circular walk encompassing the bath house and the shore.

GETTING to the ROMAN BATH HOUSE: CIRCULAR WALK or EN ROUTE to MUNCASTER CASTLE

With the shore on your left follow the road out of Ravenglass as it turns right and goes under the rail bridge and across the La'al Ratty line. Just as the road turns left, you turn right onto the broad cycleway heading into the woods. The cycleway becomes a lane and you will soon see the remains of the bath house on the left.

The bath house was built about AD130 to serve the fort of Glannoventa, which stood between the bath house and the river. The fort has melted into the trees, but parts of the bath house walls stand twelve feet high. The bath house is also known as Walls Castle.

RETURN to RAVENGLASS

If the tide is in, you will have to re-trace your steps. If the tide is out, complete the circle along the shore as follows: From the fort turn left on the lane and continue a short distance then follow the path on the right leading to the shore. The path goes under the railway line and terminates on the beach. Turn right and return to Ravenglass.

OR CONTINUE to MUNCASTER CASTLE

Turn left from the bath house. Keep left when a smaller path breaks off to the right. You will be following the Cumbrian Coastal Way. Take the second path on the left (at Newtown) and follow it to Muncaster Castle. The 1.6 mile route is quite well signposted and the path is broad throughout.

Muncaster Castle and World Owl Centre

Open Castle Su-Fr 12.00-17.00
Gardens & Owl Centre daily 10.30-18.00
Cost: Castle & Grounds: A £9.00/Ch £6.00
Grounds: A £6.00/Ch £4.00
Tel. 01229 717 614
W: www.muncaster.co.uk

GETTING to MUNCASTER CASTLE from RAVENGLASS by BUS

Bus 6,X6 d. Ravenglass rail stn car park for Muncaster Mo-Fr 3/day; Sa,Su 4/day (5 min) No BH service.

Muncaster Castle has been the home of the Penningtons since 1208. The current generations believe "the ornaments of a house are the friends who frequent it" and the thousands of annual visitors are welcomed in that spirit.

Between the entrance, where you receive a map, and the castle itself, are fabulous gardens with great billowing clouds and tumbling waves of flowers. Follow the main drive or take the high or low path through the Sino-Himalayan garden; the climate and ground at Muncaster are similar to those at 11,000 feet in the Himalayas.

The Pennington family have produced an excellent audio tour of their home. As you walk from one enthralling room to the next it will be hard to pick a favourite: the Great Hall with its elegant Alabaster Lady, the octagonal library with the exquisite miniature apprentice-made chairs, the barrel-vaulted drawing room…

GOOD EATING at MUNCASTER

Creeping Kate's Kitchen, located in the stable yard, serves home-made food to order. Tasty and a good variety.

In the grounds of the Castle you will have the chance to **Meet the Birds** at a demonstration every opening day at 14.30. These birds of prey are in the care of the World Owl Trust at Muncaster's World Owl Centre. All the birds have problems that prohibit them from surviving in the wild. You may meet Mortimer, the buzzard who is afraid of heights, and Sam the eagle owl who never learned to fly. An entertaining and thought-provoking demonstration.

Families with young children should consider the Meadow Vole Maze. This rather fun feature starts inside Max the Meadow Vole's burrow with an *incredibly* annoying little film that lasts about five minutes. Step outside the burrow into the gigantic meadow, haunt of fox, cat, badger and bees. Young children may find "nightfall in the meadow" a bit scary, but there is an emergency exit at "dusk"!

World Owl Centre, Muncaster Castle

RETURN to RAVENGLASS
Walk or Bus 6, X6 d. Muncaster

Mo-Fr 3/day; Sa,Su 4/day (5 min)
No BH service.

Days 3A & 3B – Getting Started

Both options start with the train from Whitehaven and a visit to Sellafield en route to Ravenglass (Day 3A) or Seascale for Wasdale (Day 3B).

Off peak, Sellafield is a request stop; Seascale always is. Just tell the conductor where you want to get off. To get on, wave your arm when you see the train approach.

BUS 6,X6 d. Whitehaven Duke St. for Seascale (49 min), Ravenglass (67 min) and Muncaster (71 min) Mo-Fr 3/day; Sa,Su 4/day. No BH service.

Sellafield Visitors Centre
Open daily 10.00-18.00
Cost: free
Tel. 01946 727 027

GETTING STARTED
Train d. Whitehaven for Sellafield (20 min), Seascale (for bus to Wasdale) (23 min) and Ravenglass (for hike to Wasdale) (30 min) Mo-Fr at irregular intervals of ¾-2½ hr; Sa every ¾-1¾ hr. No Sunday service
OR by BUS direct to SEASCALE, RAVENGLASS or MUNCASTER

VISITING SELLAFIELD
Telephone 01946 727 027 in the morning and tell them the time your train is due to arrive at Sellafield rail station. The Centre will send a mini-bus to pick you up. The reception staff will arrange for the bus to return you to the station for the train of your choice. There is no charge for this service.

Wastwater towards Wasdale Head

Sellafield Visitor Centre must have the friendliest and most helpful staff in England!

The main display room is all very spacious and space age: darkness illuminated by strangely glowing scattered bold shapes. Just pick a shape (they are all activities or displays) and work your way around. It really is fun!

Challenging, too. For example, put yourself in the Chernobyl control room as the reactor over-temperature alarms go off and see if you can prevent a disaster.

The Immersion Cinema presents a twenty-minute filmed debate on the future of power generation. The audience is encouraged to participate by voting on alternative solutions via touch screens at each seat.

It takes about two hours to absorb it all. Food is available in the upscale office canteen.

Days 3A and 4A continue below; days 3B and 4B continue on page 204.

Days 3A and 4A – Hike to Wasdale

DAY 3A – RAVENGLASS

CONTINUE to RAVENGLASS
from SELLAFIELD
Train d. Sellafield Mo-Fr at
irregular intervals of ¾-2½ hr;
Sa every ¾-1¾ hr (9 min)
At Ravenglass cross the footbridge and continue straight down towards the coast. Turn right along the main street. Rose Garth and Holly House are beside each other on the right.

You will have time to drop your bags at your guest house, visit Muncaster castle and explore Ravenglass.
Overnight in Ravenglass.

DAY 4A – WASDALE

This is a nice little adventure for the novice or not-particularly-serious walker. Although this route does not climb to any significant height, you will be in the fells with the distinct possibility of getting lost, so take all the standard precautions (see page 183) including the Ordnance Survey Explorer OL6 map. The hike is about five miles. Allow four hours with food breaks and discussions over the map. Take a packed lunch from your guest house or the Station Café, located on the REMR platform.

Start by taking La'al Ratty, the little train, to Dalegarth where the walk begins.

GETTING to WASDALE HEAD
and WASDALE from DALEGARTH
The following description is intended to help clarify the route,

not to replace the Ordnance Survey Explorer OL6 map. In places the route is stony, wet and very slippery.

Exit Dalegarth station and turn left into the road. Take the first road to the left for Boot. Proceed through Boot, past the mill on the right, through the wide wooden gate and follow the path uphill. When the path splits, take the route through the narrow gate. The watery sound on the right is Whillan Beck.

The large Burnmoor Tarn will appear on your left. Keep it on your left and follow the path that curves left around the far end of the tarn (the right hand path goes up Scafell Pike). The path is indistinct in places: a wide band of grass slightly more worn than that surrounding it. A few minutes after leaving the tarn, a short hill rises immediately in front of you. A distinct path leads directly up the hill, a smaller path turns left

and another turns right. Take the right hand path.

Once past Burnmoor Tarn, the path stays fairly level, with no significant hills until you start down to Fence Wood. By then you will see the wide valley of Wasdale Head.

When you reach the valley Wasdale Head is to the right. See page 187 for directions to your accommodation. For Wasdale and the Youth Hostel take either the pleasant footpath on the northwest side of Wastwater or the narrow, rocky footpath on the southeast side.

Overnight in Wasdale or Wasdale Head.

On Day 5 return to Ravenglass. You may be able to get a lift to a rail station. Otherwise retrace your steps to Dalegarth or use the taxibus to Seascale for the train (**Gosforth Taxis 019467 25308**).

Lake District Lexicon

beck, burn = stream	*knott = rocky hill*
brant = steep	*mere = lake*
dale = valley	*sca = shelter*
fell = mountain	*screes = landslip*
force = waterfall	*tarn = small mountain lake*
gill = ravine	*thwaite = clearing in woods*
how = rounded hill	*wast = lake*

Day 3B & 4B – Motor to Wasdale

DAY 3B – WASDALE

CONTINUE to WASDALE or
WASDALE HEAD from SELLAFIELD
Train d. Sellafield for Seascale
Mo-Fr at irregular intervals of ¾-
2½ hr; Sa every ¾-1¾ hr (3 min)

An infrequent taxi-bus service departs Seascale for Wasdale and Wasdale Head. The service runs only on Thursday, Saturday and Sunday and must be booked the day ahead. Since the service is informal, to say the least, verify the location of the stop and departure time when you book.

The same taxi company will do the same journey at other times and days, but costs about £14.00. Best to book this ahead as well.

For taxi and taxi-bus, telephone **Gosforth Taxis 019467 25308**.

If you need food, turn right at the rail station car park and go under the railway bridge. Ahead on the left is a grocery shop; on the right, a telephone

Overnight in Wasdale or Wasdale Head.

DAY 4B – RAVENGLASS

You may be able to get a lift to a rail station. Otherwise, take the taxi or taxi-bus to Seascale for a train. Overnight in Ravenglass.

Burnthwaite Farm at Wasdale Head

Day 5 – Proceed to Ulverston

Options A and B reunite at Ravenglass and proceed to Ulverston, in the southern part of Cumbria called the Lake District Peninsulas.

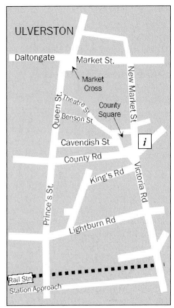

Ulverston has been a market town since receiving that status from Edward I in 1280. Outdoor markets are held on Thursday and Saturday; the indoor market, daily except Wednesday and Sunday.

To the north-east on Hoad Hill is what looks like a lighthouse but is, in fact, a monument to Sir John Barrow, a founding member of the Royal Geographical Society. If a flag is flying, the monument is open to the public. A good view of the tower is to be had from the eastbound train from Ulverston.

Stan Laurel was born on Argyle Street in 1890. The comedian and his partner are honoured at the Laurel & Hardy Museum.

An enjoyable day out from Ulverston includes a trip to Cartmel, with its medieval priory church, and to Holker Hall estate and motor museum.

A second day trip takes in Furness Abbey and the South Lakes Wild Animal Park, both close to Dalton, a short bus or train journey from Ulverston.

GETTING to ULVERSTON
Train d. Ravenglass for Barrow-in-Furness Mo-Fr at irregular intervals of ¾-2½ hr; Sa every ¾-1¾ hr (50 min).

Connecting trains d. Barrow-in-Furness for Ulverston (17 min). There are no stairs between the two platforms. No Su service.

Day 6 – Furness Abbey and Wild Animals

Furness Abbey was the second richest Cistercian abbey in England (Fountains, in Yorkshire, was the richest). It has the double advantage of a beautifully mellow location and impressively tall remains. It really is worth a visit.

The South Lakes Wild Animal Park is home for a wide range of animals representing species whose habitats and numbers are in danger. They live in conditions as natural to their own as possible and are provided with a variety of life-enriching activities to keep them healthy and happy.

From Dalton, the Wild Animal Park is a half-mile walk up a steep hill, while the abbey is about 1¾ miles in the opposite direction on the Cistercian Way. The abbey may also be reached by the same bus that travels from Ulverston to Barrow-in-Furness via Dalton.

Together they make a full-day outing with lunch in Dalton.

> GETTING to DALTON
> Bus 6,6A d. Ulverston Victoria Road for Barrow-in-Furness via Dalton Mo-Sa 4/hr; Su/BH 1/hr (11 min) This is *not* the same Bus 6 that runs to Muncaster.
> For the Wild Animal Park alight at Tudor Square, the principal stop in Dalton.

> For Furness Abbey stay on the bus a few minutes longer, or pick up a later bus from the square after visiting the Wild Animal Park.

South Lakes Wild Animal Park
Open daily 10.00-17.00
Cost: A £9.50/CoCh £6.00
Discount £1.00 with bus ticket
Tel. 01229 466 086
W: www.wildanimalpark.co.uk

> GETTING to the WILD ANIMAL PARK
> Alight Tudor Square in Dalton and look for a small brown and white sign with an elephant on it. Follow the arrow on the sign. It is a good half-mile uphill walk to the Animal Park.

The Park works to save wild animals and their habitat. Part of each admission is donated to conservation projects, and the park works with other organisations around the world with similar goals.

There is a wide range of endangered animals including, but not limited to: rhinos, hippos, lions, tigers, lemurs, spectacled bears, penguins and the largest collection of kangaroo species outside Australia. All are kept in enclosures that closely approximate their natural habitat, including mixed groupings of compatible species.

Feeding time at a zoo is always exciting, but here there is an added twist: enrichment feeding. No, they don't throw live prey to the tigers, not even obnoxious children! Instead, each meal requires natural feeding behaviour such as rooting, hunting and climbing. At the very least, the animals have to find their food, but that's not all. The tigers may have to climb a six-foot pole to get their meat, while others have to grapple with swinging baskets or root under log piles and the like. All this keeps the animals mentally and physically fit. There are feeding sessions and conservation talks throughout the day.

This is a great outing for adults and children and it contributes to a good cause.

Furness Abbey (EH)
Open daily Apr-Sep10.00-18.00
Oct 10.00-16.00
Cost: A £3.00/Co £2.30/Ch £1.50
Tel. 01229 823 420

GETTING to FURNESS ABBEY
Bus 6 and 6A have almost identical routes, diverging briefly in the area of the abbey. Bus 6A will take you closer. Whichever bus you take, ask to be let down close to Abbey House Hotel. Ask the driver to point the direction to the hotel and before alighting, ask where to pick up the return bus. While many country buses respond to a hopeful wave by stopping, the Barrow-Ulverston buses do not and it is an all-uphill walk back to Dalton.

You are looking for Abbey Approach, a small lane that diverges from the main road and passes under a red sandstone arch a few metres closer to Dalton than Abbey House Hotel. Walk downhill less than 5 minutes to the abbey entrance.

As you approach the abbey you will pass through the main gatehouse into the Vale of Deadly Nightshade, just as visitors did over 800 years ago.

Furness Abbey started life in 1127 as a Savigniac monastery, the first in England. Twenty years later the Savigniac order merged with the Cistercians, but the abbot of Furness, Peter of York, resisted the merger. He eventually yielded to pressure and resigned when his abbey accepted Cistercian rule in 1150.

Over the next four centuries the abbey grew in prosperity and importance, in spite of its isolated position. Never kid yourself the abbots used their extraordinary power for the good of the population. Furness Abbey increased its sheep-grazing capacity by destroying inconveniently located villages. Maybe enforced relocation is good for the soul.

In common with many houses of the Cistercian order, Furness suffered a decline in the fourteenth century and never regained its position. It surrendered to the commissioners of Henry VIII in 1537. For more about the Cistercians, see page 53.

The price of admission includes an audio tour of the site. A full history of the abbey is presented in the visitor centre together with several grave covers and stonework from the abbey.

RETURN to ULVERSTON
From the location indicated by your outbound bus driver or back at Tudor Square in Dalton, pick up bus 6,6A for the return trip to Ulverston Mo-Sa 4/hr; Su/BH 1/hr

Day 7 – Cark (Holker Hall) and Cartmel

From Ulverston it is one train stop east to Cark & Cartmel, a single rail station that serves two villages. Don't forget to look out for the monument on Hoad Hill as the train leaves Ulverston.

The stately house and gardens of Holker Hall are just one mile from Cark. The Hall is full of entrancing features and wonderful stories told by the room stewards. The Lakeland Motor Museum is here also.

Cartmel is a pleasant walk of about 2¼ miles from the station. A bus runs from the centre of Cark to Cartmel Monday to Saturday. The focal point of Cartmel is the Priory Church of St. Mary and St. Michael, but its real claim to fame is its sticky toffee pudding. Plan you day's activities around sampling some of this – with custard, of course!

GETTING to CARK
Train d. Ulverston to Cark & Cartmel Mo-Sa every ¾-1¾ hr; Su every 2-3½ hr (8 min) Cross the footbridge over the railway and turn right at the road. You will very soon come to the village of Cark.

Cartmel

From Cark, you can proceed to the medieval village of Cartmel, either by bus or on foot.

GETTING to CARTMEL by BUS
Bus 532 d. Cark opposite the Engine Inn for Cartmel Mo-Sa 4/day (7 min)

Holker Hall sun dial lets you calculate the time with great accuracy.

or by FOOT

From the centre of Cark continue along the main road out of the village, keeping to the right when it splits. There is a tiny sign on the wall: "Cartmel 2".

At the top of the hill, about 5 minutes from the village centre, look out on your left for an unmarked narrow lane that may be barred by a metal gate. Proceed through the gate and follow the lane. (If you miss the turn you will walk another 10 to 15 minutes into open countryside before seeing a farm set well back from the road on the left. The lane to the farm is sign-posted as a bridleway. Follow the lane through the farm and turn right at the top, which puts you on the correct route.)

The lane terminates at a T-junction. Turn right and follow the main path (ignore a smaller path that turns left into the woods) across the race course and car park and into Cartmel. Total walk about 45 min.

Cartmel is one of the oldest and prettiest of Cumbria's villages. It grew around the priory, which was established in 1189 at the request of one William Marshal for the purpose of having thirteen monks pray for his soul and those of his family in perpetuity – a sort of after-life insurance policy.

There are little shops, galleries, inns and cafés around the market square and down the alleys. Cartmel also has a racecourse with flat racing held on the spring and summer bank holiday weekends.

The Priory Church of St. Mary and St. Michael

Open daily 9.00-17.30 except during services
Cost: free

The church was built as part of the Augustinian priory founded in 1189. It remained isolated with only occasional visits by church authorities. As a response to attacks by Scots in 1316 and 1322, the gatehouse was strengthened and still stands.

The monks of Cartmel resisted the dissolution of their priory by Henry VIII. As a result, several monks and villagers were hanged for treason. The church itself, although stripped of valuables, was saved because the villagers claimed it as their parish church.

The Prestons of Holker Hall were responsible for much of the post-dissolution restoration of the building. About 300 years later, the Duke of Devonshire, the Victorian owner of Holker Hall and descendant of the Prestons, also made a significant contribution to the repair of the church.

The church retains much of its

original Norman structure with Decorated and Perpendicular additions. The chancel, where the main altar is located, is flanked by two choirs, which, in this context, means an enclosed space. The south (right hand) choir was possibly used by the villagers of Cartmel as their parish church. The north choir, which is the oldest part of the church, was once a small chapel and is now called the Piper Choir.

Although the church and the gatehouse are all that remain of the priory buildings, there are clues to its past.

You can still see the upper part of the night stairs leading to a blocked doorway. These gave the monks quick access from their dormitory to the choir for their night services.

The fancifully carved little seats in the 15[th]C choir are misericords, designed so the monks could rest their bottoms on the narrow seat, but if they fell asleep the hinged seat would flip down with a bang.

More recently, four sculptures by Josefina de Vasconcellos have been installed.

As always with ancient churches, look for the details of stone and wood carvings – they are often full of wonderful surprises.

210

Don't be alarmed if you see a procession of short monks heading for the chancel and prostrating themselves in front of the altar – they are local school children on a learning experience!

Finally, have a look at the church tower. The upper portion is rotated 45° with respect to the lower. For more information on monasteries, see page 46.

Cartmel Priory Gatehouse (NT)

Open We-Su/BH 10.00-16.00.
Closed on all Cartmel Race days
Cost: A £2.00/Ch 50p
Tel. 01524 701 178

The priory gatehouse was used as a grammar school from 1624 to 1790 and is now run as a heritage centre for Cartmel village and peninsula.

RETURN to CARK by BUS
Bus 532 d. Cartmel for Cark Mo-Sa 4/day (6 min)

Holker Hall & Lakeland Motor Museum

Open Hall Su-Fr 10.30-16.45
Gardens Su-Fr 10.30-17.30
Motor Museum daily 10.30-14.45
Cost: Tickets are sold for just about any combination of house, gardens and motor museum. The cost for the 'All In' ticket is A £9.25/Ch £5.50
Holker Hall
Tel. 015395 58328
www.holker-hall.co.uk

Motor Museum
Tel. 015395 58509
www.lakelandmotormuseum.co.uk

Cartmel Priory owned the land on which Holker Hall now stands. After the dissolution, the property was bought by the Preston family, but it was not until 1610 that the family moved to the site.

Almost 400 years later, having been passed from generation to generation, Holker Hall is now the home of Lord and Lady Cavendish. The Hall is very much a family home, and exploring it is particularly enjoyable due to a lack of ropes holding the peasantry away from the furniture!

You can wander around the rooms on the understanding that you don't touch anything. The house is full of tactile temptations and the itch to stroke the worn leather book bindings, the polished limestone arches, the silk wallpaper and the marble tables is strong.

In particular, examine the woodwork: it is hand-carved throughout the house. As is usual with such work, there are hidden goodies in the carvings: for example, almost immediately ahead when you enter you will see a frieze just above a Chinese chest. You should be able to decipher a name and date. A lovely portrait of the person in question hangs over the cantilevered staircase. (While this type of staircase is aesthetically pleasing, it puts a huge stress on the walls. As at Durham Castle, a supporting column had to be added to prevent the staircase from pulling the house down around itself.) Room stewards will fill you in on the history of the family and the furniture of the Hall.

The grounds offer everything from the formal Elliptical and Summer Gardens to a wildflower meadow. There is a particularly exquisite and unexpected vista featuring two herons. This alone put Holker Hall in my Enchanted Garden category!

Walk further into the fields to see the Holker Hall Sundial. It is shaped from Blue Grey Lakeland Slate and is scientific work of art.

The **Lakeland Motor Museum** is an interesting collection of cars, motor cycles and related items. The highlight, for the adults at least, is the collection of 50-year old mechanical games. Put your 10p or 20p in the slot and play

Part of the enchanted garden at
Holker Hall

soccer, steer a racing car or guide
your coin through a maze to the re-
turned-coin slot for a refund.

GOOD EATING

The Courtyard Café offers a range
of excellent salads, soups, sandwiches and hot meals, all made
from estate or local produce. It
isn't cheap but is good value for
money - £7.25 for a salmon and
crabmeat salad that was worth
every penny!

RETURN to ULVERSTON

Train d. Cark & Cartmel for Ulverston. Mo-Sa every ¾-1¾ hr; Su
every 2–3½ hr (8 min)

Getting Home

From Ulverston you can proceed
directly to Lancaster or Manchester Piccadilly for mainline trains,
or continue to Manchester airport.

Trains depart Ulverston Monday to Saturday every ¾ to 1¾
hours and every 2 to 3½ hours on
Sunday.

*If Wasdale = the valley with a
lake,
does Wastwater = a lake with
water in it?
See Lake District Lexicon on page
203 for more wonderful words.*

Acknowledgements

Photographs on pages 21, 22, 52, 57, 61 and 84 provided by **Regia Anglorum**, an international society based in the UK. Their 600+ members seek to accurately recreate the lives of the inhabitants of the Islands of Britain a thousand years ago. Their Living History Exhibit demonstrates many everyday activities. A common sense and safe system of weapon instruction is in use. They own and operate five full-scale ship replicas and are building a permanent site near Canterbury in South Eastern England. For more information email **contact@regia.org** or visit **www.regia.org**

Photographs on pages 120, 133 and 193 provided by **Legio Secunda Augusta**. LEGIIAVG and associated group Ludus Gladiatorius are voluntary groups with a passion for reconstructing the archaeology of the first and second centuries AD, whether military, civilian or gladiator. Working with archaeologists, historians, engineers, costumiers, artists and enthusiasts, the group, which numbers well over one hundred members throughout Britain, Europe and even the USA, regularly presents at archaeological sites across the continent. The group also regularly features on film and television. For information, visit **www.ludus.org.uk** or **www.legiiavg.org.uk**

The National Trust

Founded in 1895 for the preservation of places of historic interest or natural beauty, the National Trust is a registered charity (no. 205846) whose work is supported by members' subscriptions. Their work includes preserving historic homes and gardens, stately and otherwise, and protecting and maintaining large tracts of countryside and coast. Many of the properties and much of the countryside included in *Local Routes* tours are accessible for our enjoyment due to the National Trust.

Benefits of membership include the annual Handbook, free admission to the properties listed in the Handbook, three editions of the superb National Trust magazine and two editions of a regional newsletter. You can join at a National Trust property or shop, by telephone at:
0870 458 4000 or online at:
www.nationaltrust.org.uk/join

English Heritage

Established by Act of Parliament in 1984, English Heritage protects and promotes England's historic environment. It advises the Government on what should be protected and is involved in research, archiving and education. It manages over 400 historic sites and publishes excellent property guides and history books. English Heritage receives income from a government grant, but depends heavily on its commercial activities, membership subscriptions, donations and visitors to the properties in its care.

Benefits of membership include the annual handbook, free admission to English Heritage properties (children up to 18 years may enter free when accompanied by a member), reduced admission to over 100 other historic attractions and a quarterly magazine. Join at an English Heritage property, by telephone at:
0870 333 1182 or online at:
www.english-heritage.org.uk

NOTES

USEFUL TELEPHONE NUMBERS & WEB SITES

General Tourist Information
Tel. 0208 563 3186
W: www.visitbritain.com

Traveline: 0870 608 2 608

National Rail Enquiries
Tel. 08457 48 49 50
W: www.nationalrail.co.uk

GNER information and ticket sales
Tel. 08457 225 225
W: www.gner.co.uk

Northern Rail customer service
Tel. 0845 00 00 125
W: www.northernrail.org

TransPennine Express Customer
Service: Tel. 0845 600 1671
W: www.tpexpress.co.uk

Virgin Trains information and ticket
sales: Tel. 08457 222 333
W: www.virgintrains.co.uk